MONTAHA HIDEFI

GIVING VOICE TO MY SILENCE

My Struggle for Respect from Venezuela to Syria

First published in 2022 by OC Publishing
Halifax, NS, Canada, www.ocpublishing.ca

Cover concept by Montaha Hidefi, www.montahahidefi.ca

Book design and interior layout by Creation Booth Limited, www.creationbooth.com

Cover photography by Breila Von Holstein-Rathlou, Breila Rose

All rights reserved under international copyright conventions. No part of this publication may be reproduced, stored in, or introduced into a retrieval system, or transmitted in any form or by any means, without the prior written permission of the author.

ISBN - 978-1-989833-19-3 (Paperback Edition)
ISBN - 978-1-989833-21-6 (eBook Edition)

Copyright © 2022 Montaha Hidefi

Dedication

To all who muted their voices for fear of speaking.

May the voice I am giving to my silence be an inspirational wind chime that will encourage you to break your silence and allow it to have a voice.

Montaha Hidefi

Prologue

Has it ever occurred to you to stop everything you are doing for an instant and ask yourself how much courage it would take to step outside the line dividing you, the leading character of your life performance, and others, the spectators watching you performing your own play on the theatre of life? How about taking on the role of the narrator instead of being part of the narrative?

In recent years, I came to understand that there are two sorts of narratives: those that remain unspoken and repressed; and those that unexpectedly resurface after years of suppression to bite us in the face. Some of the latter, when exposed, may cause embarrassment. Some others are like an Erlenmeyer flask filled with human excrement. When the stopper is removed, the shame of the offensive odour it emits will last a generation.

To assume the role of the narrator is to become the spectator and to strip all narratives from their veneers, one layer at a time, and scan the microscopic particles concealed inside the peaks and valleys of the ripples. As your own narrator, you undertake the responsibility to stand tall and be ready to accept the consequences, no matter how unforgiving.

For most of my life, while performing as the main character in my play, I was incapable of taking a seat in the auditorium. But I managed to become a spectator of my own drama when I decided to put an end to my silence, out of fear of being disbelieved or ridiculed, and give it a voice.

Now, three years after the publication of *Groping for Truth: My Uphill Struggle for Respect*, I feel liberated from the burden that weighed on me. I can now rest in the middle of the auditorium and watch the gloomy, past events of my life parading dramatically on the stage after the curtains are opened to announce the beginning of the show.

The idea of sharing my stories through a book started years before *Groping for Truth* was published, but I had neither the time nor the courage to accept this challenge. By the time

I turned fifty, I wanted to give myself a gift and decided to start writing. Then, just as I started to write, I lost my job and had to drop the project while searching for another, which led to my move to Canada. It was not until the end of 2017, with the influence of the Me-Too movement, which allowed many people to un-silence their voices without being ridiculed, that I was inspired to resume the writing process.

This movement, as well as the brave women that have come forth to disclose their dreadful experiences with sexual misconduct or abuse by Hollywood stars, high-profile leaders, and men at all levels in the workplace and everywhere else, has ignited a fire in me I thought was extinguished long ago and banished to the inner caves of my psyche.

I started paying more attention to the news related to sexual misbehaviour. For the first time, as far back as I could remember, married, divorced, and single women of all ages and backgrounds were gathering the courage to overcome the humiliation and shame of disclosing stories of sexual violations perpetrated against them.

With each story I heard, a new chamber in my inner caves was unsealed, reminding me of an unsolicited event I had laid to rest in the darkness of a profound precipice I thought I would never access again. I felt disturbed.

Each evening, as I went to bed and laid my head on the pillow, the stories replayed in my mind's eye. These were followed by a dialogue between my present and my past. "What are you going to do?" the present asked. "Nothing," the past said. "Many of these stories happened long ago, and some of their antagonists might have died already, so what are the benefits of disclosing them?"

I was torn between the Me that got used to concealing stories for fear of adverse repercussions and the Me that was seeing an opportunity to eventually release the shame of those moments that happened at times and places when people exercised their power and authority over me.

I felt restless for several days and nights. Then, soon after my birthday, on the second week of January of 2018, a friend of mine named Karl paid us a visit. I got to know Karl in 2010 as a co-worker. We have held a mutually respectful relationship since the first time we met. After I discovered his interest in music, I suggested we go out for dinner, so he could meet my husband who is a musician and songwriter. At dinner, they exchanged stories about music. After we finished dining, my husband invited him home to show his musical instruments. Karl and I were having a conversation about Harvey Weinstein and the sexual harassment allegations.

"If I only spoke about my own experiences, I could probably write a book," I said.

His reaction was: "You should! But I could only imagine how painful that would be for you."

He was correct. I have suppressed those events from my memory, not only because of the humiliation they caused me when they happened, but also because of the emotional state of mind they put me in then. Bringing them to the fore would be a challenging process.

The topic lingered in my mind for days, and against all odds, one evening during the last week of January, while sitting in front of the television listening to more news about sexual misconduct, I unlocked my iPad, clicked on the Notes app, and started listing the incidents that sprang up in my mind like popcorn bursting inside a microwave.

"My goodness," I said aloud. "I could really write a book!"

To my surprise, my husband, Michael, who was sitting next to me, encouraged me, saying, "You should!"

The level of distress and the feeling of solidarity with the women coming forward as they were roaring "Enough is enough!" convinced me that silence was never a remedy to any gaping wound and that it was about time for me to unbolt the gates to the shameful stories that lay deep down in the abyss, so they could at last leave me to become public knowledge. Not out of pride, but to wipe the humiliating scars of a shame only a person that has been through the same experience could understand.

I recognized then that once I initiated such a venture, there was no going back and that it might come back to bite me hard.

Following an exhaustive self-deliberation, I made the decision to be brave and face my reservations. Encouraged by the favourable circumstances to at last give voice to my silence, I decided to recount the untold stories of the numerous layers of physical abuse and sexual misbehaviour I was exposed to throughout my childhood, youth, and mature age, how I dealt with each of them, what I learned, and how they had affected and influenced me. Some of these stories might sound humorous, some others might make you think of a similar incident you have heard of or lived yourself. Whatever your reaction, know that the process of poking a hole in the drapes of my past to retrieve these memories, long crushed by countless thin sheets of heavy metal, is one filled with anxiety, shame, and embarrassment.

As I typed the outline for each unsolicited occurrence revealed in this book, I became conscious of a reality I did not anticipate when I made the choice to assume the role of the narrator of my stories. Every time I typed the first person pronoun "I" to start a sentence, I felt a large amount of pressure being placed upon me, as if a thousand-ton steel block were pushing on my chest, cutting off my breath, and producing an intense anxiety.

The magnitude of feelings was such that after I did the outline and wanted to start writing the first stories, I felt powerless. A feeling of paralysis overcame me. My fingers were incapable of striking the letter "I" on my keyboard to describe and portray myself in certain situations, at certain times, being the subject of certain actions. I could not write! I had to stop.

For 10 consecutive days I separated myself from the first pages I had written, thinking that this project had failed. I did not think of continuing to write. I could not do it!

Then, on the tenth night, as I laid my head on the pillow, I closed my eyes and emitted a long deep sigh. An abrupt ray of light radiated behind my eyelids, followed by a clear concept. If I were unable to report the events in the first person, I could disclose them in the third person, transforming the Me from being the subject "I" to Me becoming the object "She," which would hopefully ease the fluttering of the butterflies in my stomach. I felt that I had been struck by a mystical lightning and that I had finally found my way through it all. I smiled and fell asleep soon after.

Next morning, I clicked the document open and resumed the narration in the third person. As I started referring to myself as a character called Monti, which is my nickname, I planned to distance myself from the embarrassment and shame produced by telling the stories.

After having drafted the first 30 pages, I submitted the manuscript to my publisher, Anne Louise O'Connell, for feedback. She suggested that the reader's experience would be richer if I told the stories in the first person. It was already too overwhelming to narrate in the third person; I was certain I could not write a sentence in the first person and re-experience the pain caused by the incidents a second time, even if that meant a better reader experience.

I stopped writing again!

A month passed during which I reflected over the entire process of drafting the book and whether it was worth it to go through the distress caused by invoking distant memories.

One morning, as the wilful woman I have always known myself to be, I clicked open the document and started writing. When I typed the first "I," I had a feeling of being stabbed in the heart, and a string of blood started dripping inside of me. By the time I had written it several times, I was sitting in a pond of thick red matter, but I continued writing. I had to overcome the suffering to convey my stories with courage, with the anticipation of transforming the obscure calamities of the past into a shining light for the future.

I thank the individuals that had the courage before me to speak up and denounce what has always been a stigma for us to talk about. It helped make my decision to write about my experiences. While recognizing the repercussions this book might have on my life, and because most of my stories happened long ago, I have, in some cases, been unable to remember the names of the antagonists or did not know their names at all. Although my initial decision was to use pseudonyms to refer to those that violated my confidence, as I progressed in the writing process, I reconsidered and decided not to allow the abuse to continue by hiding their names. So, all the names I mention are real.

This book is dedicated to anyone who has silently suffered from physical, online, psychological, or sexual abuse, sexual harassment, or any other type of abusive behaviour in their lives. It is my intention to share my stories, no matter how painful this process has been, with the hope that it will encourage the silenced, wherever they are around the world, to come forth, give voice to their silence, and know that they are not alone. Now, in any present time, is the right time to put an end to our, until now, muted grief and expose its true colours.

If silence had a colour, what colour would it be?

If silence had a voice, what colour would that voice be?

My silence was muted, gloomy, and impenetrable. Colourless!

But the voice I grant it today displays the colours of the rainbow. When this voice expresses anger or rebellion, its colour is red, like the blood in my veins. When it manifests freedom, it is blue, like the free waters of the oceans. When it reflects optimism for a better tomorrow, it is yellow, like the sun's rays, and when it reveals fear and depression, it is black as darkness.

I included these colours in the cover of this book to symbolize the message I want to convey. The title is red, the text on the cover is yellow, there is blue in my outfit, and I used black as the backdrop.

The cover colours truly represent the journey of coming out of the darkness into the light as I confer various hues to my silence, because the frequency of each colour defines a different situation. What is the colour you will confer to the voice of your silence?

Chapter 1

On Wednesday, July 25, 2018, I received sad news from friends and family living in the province of Al-Sweida in Syria. During the early hours of the morning, a terrorist cell of the Islamic State Daesh had attacked eastern villages of the province, resulting in the death of 250 men and women and the wounding of hundreds more as they were trying to protect their land.

The news was disturbing and worrying. Although I am a Canadian citizen, I was born in Venezuela to a Syrian immigrant family. Many of my family members and dear friends still reside in Al-Sweida.

In 1945, Syria emerged as an independent country, effectively ending France's occupation of its territory. Much like today, albeit for varied reasons, those were tough times of conflicts, political and economic unrest in Syria. Thousands of young Syrian men and women migrated to Venezuela during the oil boom of the 1950s, seeking a better life. Today, it is presumed that over a million Venezuelans are of Syrian descent, and it is said that 60 percent of Al-Sweida's population are born in Venezuela and carry dual nationality.

Father arrived in Venezuela in 1957, three years before I was born. His brother, Tio Salman, migrated there a year or two earlier. They were born in Al-Kafr, a small village perched in the mountainous region of Al-Sweida. Al-Sweida is Arabic for black and an allusion to the dark volcanic terrain.

Tio Salman was part of our daily lives. He exhumed empathy, always wore a smile, and had a good sense of humour. He had a special affection for me and called me by another of my nicknames, Negra. He often visited with his wife and three children: two girls, and a boy, named Nazih but nicknamed Domingo. They lived in El Tigre in the state of Anzoátegui, as we did. I do not remember when or how specifically it began, but Tio Salman started mentioning that I had been promised to be Domingo's, my first cousin's, bride.

It is quite customary for an Arabic family to promise their young daughters for marriage to whomever they see fit, whether it is due to family ties, the conservation of the bloodline, or for financial benefits. Many young girls grow up being told who their future husband will be. The groom-to-be is most often a relative. In other cases, he could be the son of a neighbour or a friend of the family.

Mother also had an arranged marriage. I can still remember how distressing it was to all of us, many years ago, when she told us the story of how it happened.

She recollected that one evening in 1951 or 1952, before villagers held records of such events, a young man in his early twenties, accompanied by his parents, paid a visit to her family at the east end of Al-Kafr. The visit's purpose was to ask for her hand in marriage. She was only 15.

She recounted that when she overheard the visitors speaking in the next room that ill-fated evening, as she called it, and realized the purpose of the visit, she was scared. She cautiously snuck downstairs to the pantry. It was pitch-black, as there was no electricity in the village then. She climbed into an empty burlap potato sack that was resting on the dirty floor and fell asleep.

Hours later, she was abruptly awakened by brutal kicks to her side. It was her father! He had been looking for her and finally discovered her secret hiding place in the potato sack. She burst out of the sack disturbed and apprehensive. Her father demanded that she follow him upstairs. As a spiritual leader, her father was notorious in Al-Kafr for being a fearsome, religious man that everybody respected. She obeyed his orders.

As they reached the family room upstairs, he announced she was to marry Hassan, son of Sulaiman, in the upcoming months. She felt her world crumble! She was cold and hungry having spent the evening in a potato sack in the dark, damp pantry.

Giving Voice to My Silence

Suddenly, she found her voice, picked from the leftovers of her cowardice, and said, "I do not want to marry him! I do not like him!"

Furious at her insubordination, her father brought his arms forward and squeezed his fists together, as if he were wringing a chicken's neck. "If you don't marry him," he said, "I'll snap your neck like a chicken! Do you understand?"

There was nothing left to say or do. Mother's fate had been decided while she hid in the pantry. As she recounted, she was so horrified, she let her head sink forward to avoid eye contact with her father and walked away wordlessly. That night, she could not sleep at all. She felt powerless. All she could do was stare in the hollow darkness of the room as her pupils grew wider.

After hearing Mother's arranged marriage story, I had feelings of abhorrence toward my grandfather and thought I was fortunate I did not meet him, as he died when I was a child.

Although both Mother and Father were descendants of House Hidefi, they were not related by any bloodline, as Father descended from clan Hamad and Mother from clan Nakad.

Following the footsteps of the women in her family, Mother never attended school. She was illiterate and uneducated. Schools were not meant to be attended by females. Females were predestined to marry as early as possible to procreate, address the matters of their in-laws in whose house they lived with their husbands, and functioned as domestic help.

Because of her lack of education, Mother was not an intellectually nimble girl; she was ill-informed about the world surrounding her as well as life in general. She never heard of menstruation until she menstruated a year after she got married while living with her in-laws.

Two years after her marriage, when she gave birth to her first daughter, my eldest sister, Tanahe, nicknamed Danela, her mother-in-law taught her how to breastfeed and manage the baby's diapers. Father was not involved with the baby's upbringing. A man's key role was to provide for his family.

As those were times of scarcity and shortage of everything following Syria's liberation from the French mandate, to be able to feed his family, Father found a job as a clerk at Al-Sweida Hotel in the city of Damascus, capital of Syria. He visited the household at the end of each month to bring the earnings. He was a timid young man, yet his secondary school education helped him to get the front-desk clerk job at the hotel, where he also resided.

My cousin Domingo was a year or two older than me. We often played together during weekend gatherings. Although he was a shy boy, after a tropical rainy day, we used to pick worms in the front yard and build mud houses for them. He had big, round, greenish-brown eyes, encircled by a dark ring, and a deep-chocolate complexion from exposure to the equatorial sun.

As a child, I was unable to perceive the notion of being a bride. I thought of Domingo as a brother. Tio Salman's insinuations of an impending marriage often made me uncomfortable, something I was unable to explain or grasp.

In 1964, my family, then with five girls, relocated to San Fernando de Apure in the state of Apure in the southwest planes of Venezuela on the Apure River, where most of the Syrian community was relocating in search of a better financial life. Domingo and I were separated geographically as, at the same time, Tio Salman had repatriated his family back to Syria. This did not prevent Tio Salman and other family friends, then all living in San Fernando, from expecting us to marry. As soon as he would enter the house, Tio Salman would yell with such enthusiasm and eagerness, "Where's the Negra, Domingo's bride?" to such an extent that my uneasiness developed into hatred for my cousin, even though I did not understand why.

In Middle Eastern cultures, young girls' exposure to such allusions during their childhood is to prepare them early on to become mothers to ensure the family's legacy. For me, it was

Giving Voice to My Silence

as if the family were conditioning me to accept an unacceptable act. However, in my underdeveloped brain, the more I was exposed to the brainwashing, the more I ignored the idea of ever becoming Domingo's, or anyone else's, bride.

The indoctrination practice, whether intentionally or unintentionally, was having a conflicting effect on me. Every time Tio Salman mentioned Domingo, my heart pounded fast, and I could feel the blood rising to my temples, emitting a stinging, burning metal smell in my head. I would look down at my toes, run as fast as I could toward the kitchen, and hold my chest with my little hand to prevent my heart from falling to the ground. I did not understand what I was feeling.

I took refuge in the dark kitchen that I dreaded even though I was terrified, Tio Salman would pull me out and cuddle me in his arms with much affection. I would force a smile to hide my fear and timidly tell him, "I don't want to be a bride!" He would laugh and say, "Of course you do!" His intimidating insinuations felt like hundred-pound weights crushing my chest.

After moving to San Fernando, Father owned and ran a mid-size variety store. The store was connected to the house on the corner of Paez and Ayacucho Streets. The property was an old church converted into a house. The store had big, rolling metal front doors with rusted edges. From the house, the store was accessed through the master bedroom, which later became the kids' room after another extension was added to the house. In it, Father carried an assortment of fabrics such as batiste, flannel, rayon, trevira, and polyester.

The batiste rolls came in soft pastels and were smooth to the touch. The flannels had white backgrounds and small floral prints. They were used to make pyjamas due to their soft, almost velvety feel. The treviras had bigger floral patterns and came in hues of brown, yellow, green, and dark red with accents of lilac, soft blue, and white.

My passion for colour must have started then, as I always admired the colours and patterns of the textiles. The store also carried an assortment of ready-made clothing and accessories such as nylons, buttons, zippers, fasteners, underwear, and even shoes.

Although Father worked hard to support our family, the business did not generate much income. The earnings were just enough to pay the rent and utilities and buy food. We did not have a washing machine or other appliances except for a cooking range and a refrigerator. Mother did the laundry by hand and used a rope strung in the open-plan garage to dry everything. She also sewed our outfits with an old, black Singer sewing machine. We carried a simple life and lived below a normal standard.

Chapter 2

One scorching summer evening in San Fernando, in August of 1965, Mother went out to buy *caracol*, a mosquito-repelling incense, and a *refresco*, a soda, to quench her thirst. She asked me to accompany her.

The *quincallería*, hardware store, which sold caracol was at the other end of the block, five minutes away. The *bodega* selling the drinks was another 5 to 10 minutes farther down the road on Santa Ana Street. As we reached the entrance of the quincallería, a black hearse, followed by many cars, passed by in a funeral procession. It was not the first time I witnessed a funeral procession. However, for mysterious reason, this one piqued my curiosity. We entered the quincallería and Mother ordered the caracol from Mr. Chung, the owner. Mr. Chung fetched a green package and placed it on the counter.

I asked, *"Chino, ¿quién se murió?"* Hey, Chinaman, who died?

Mr. Chung was infuriated by my question, he picked the package off the counter and chucked it at my face, yelling, *"¡Tu misma!"* You did!

The force of the package hitting me was so strong it propelled me backwards. I did not understand Mr. Chung's reaction to my innocent question. All I wanted to know was who had died. I did not know then that calling him "Chino," as we referred to him at home, was a racial slur.

I picked the caracol package from the floor where it landed and threw it back at him with all my might. I quickly turned toward the door and said to Mother, *"¡Vámonos!"* Let's move!, and ran out of the store. I did not look back and never set foot again in Mr. Chung's quincallería. Mother, who was expecting to give birth to her sixth child at any moment, followed me out, feeling embarrassed and confused.

I scampered down the sidewalk, shaking with fury. Mother yelled for me to slow down. When she reached my side, she demanded an explanation. I could not deliver one. All I knew was that Mr. Chung went too far in mistreating a five-year-old child because I asked him an innocent question.

We continued walking in silence until we reached the bodega. Mother was tired, her legs were swollen, and her overhanging, pregnant belly almost touched her thighs. She allowed her heavy body to rest on the tightly woven, red rubber of the Scoubidou chair outside the bodega and ordered two bottles of Orange Hit, which was the name of Fanta in Venezuela. We sat in silence sipping our refrescos, Mother looking distressed. The bodega did not sell caracol, and she desperately needed it to repel the relentless mosquitos.

On the way back home, Mother was exhausted. By then, I was in a better mood and told her I would get the caracol next morning from another bodega.

When I got up the next morning, I could not find Mother. I ran towards my parents' bedroom, at the back of the store. The door was open. I stepped in and saw Mother lying in bed, looking weary, with an irregular-shaped, light blue bulge like a bursting burlap bag on her right side. I stopped, confused. Mother asked that I come to her. I walked slowly until I reached the bedside. She uncovered the bulge to reveal the face of a little, sleepy baby.

"Last night, while everybody was deeply asleep, a white stork came in from the skies and dropped your brother on my bed," she said. "Can you see how beautiful he is?"

Perplexed, I glanced at the baby to make sure his face was not smashed by the drop. It was the first time I had seen a baby boy, and he was my brother.

I delicately leaned forward to have a better look at him and smelled the pleasant scent of baby talcum emanating from this cherubic creature. His face was not smashed. On the contrary, he was sleeping like an angel.

"Your brother's name is Sulaiman," Mother whispered, "but we will call him Hacinto."

In Arab cultures, bringing forth a male offspring used to be, and continues to be in many societies, the ultimate and

Giving Voice to My Silence

most significant goal of a couple. Males carry forward the clan's heritage and preserve their House's name through history and time.

Despite their dreadful economic condition, my parents continued having children with the hope of bearing a male child. Hacinto was the sixth child. Mother was shunned by her in-laws for bringing to life five consecutive females. Outrageously, they looked upon her as been of an inferior reproductive bloodline. She felt under pressure to keep reproducing until she had a male, even if that meant a dozen children.

My elder sisters, Danela, and Yusra were in Syria when Hacinto was born. Two years earlier, they were sent to Syria in the company of Tio Salman's family. Father felt it would be best for them to spend time with our grandparents in Al-Kafr and attend school to learn Arabic. Soon after Hacinto's birth, Danela and Yusra returned to San Fernando, as they were considered a burden and a liability the family in Al-Kafr did not want to deal with. In addition, Mother needed help to cope with the baby, the other children, Father, and the store.

To earn enough money to put food on the table for a large family, Father purchased an industrial sewing machine, installed it at the back of the store, and learned how to produce *cauchos*, ponchos. The cauchos were made of synthetic black leather, sometimes brown, two metres square in size, and were destined for the *vaqueros*, cowboys, to wear while working the ranches and riding their horses in the rainy season. To help Father, Danela and Yusra also learned how to sew and worked hard next to him.

The arrival of Hacinto changed things at home, especially for me. I noticed that Father treated him differently from the way he treated us girls. He bought Hacinto little toys, and once he started walking, Father started taking him to the *abasto*, supermarket, an activity that was not customary for us girls. During the journeys to the abasto, Hacinto could have whatever he wanted, no matter the price.

On one occasion, Hacinto came back from the abasto with a cluster of white, shiny things in his hand. "What's this?" I asked. "Grapes," he replied.

Venezuela was not known for growing grapes. At the age of eight, I had never seen or tasted grapes. The white, greenish, transparent colour of the fruits looked so appealing to the eye and enticing to the palate, I wanted to touch the skin of the grapes and savour one. Hacinto was extremely generous, and he gave me two or three grapes. I took the grapes in my right hand, my intense look almost penetrating their delicate skin. I brought my hand under my nose and took a deep sniff.

Although I did not know what mowed lawn smelled, the soft, earthy scent brought sensations of freshly trimmed, green grass, which made me think I was in the park down the road, where I used to play. I waited a long while before inserting the first grape into my mouth. I closed my eyes and lifted my tongue up, smashing the grape against the roof of my mouth. The delicate skin of the grape shattered under my palate's pressure, allowing the sweet pulp to disperse onto my taste buds. I was thrown into a place I never knew existed, a garden of flavours and colours. I would never forget that instant; I fell in love with grapes that day.

Later, I started improvising tactics to obtain a share of the goodies Hacinto was bringing from the abasto. I seized the notion that being a boy was different than being a girl. Being a boy meant being taken to the abasto, being gifted a variety of fruits not usually accessible to girls, being gifted a tricycle, being dressed, and scented differently, and being loved differently.

It would not be wrong to presume those were the days that set the foundation for my rivalry, and further rebellion, against my brother and parents.

My rebellion against the family's new living conditions began exhibiting itself first with unfriendly behaviour that escalated into hostility against my little brother.

I could not understand why Hacinto was receiving better treatment than me. No one at home was concerned about me or my feelings, and I never received an explanation. The more affection Mother and Father wrapped Hacinto with, the more rejected I felt and the more hard-headed I became. I was so envious of Hacinto that all I wanted was to get rid of him or become a boy like him.

One day, I was so upset because Hacinto did not want to share with me a bar of chocolate, I ran after him around the backyard, bearing a metal squeegee in my hands. He was running in front of me shouting for help. By the time Mother came to the rescue, I had knocked him on the head.

It was a minor cut, but the bleeding had alarmed the entire family. Mother, storming and menacing, shouted, *"Enagsek ala oumrik!"* May you be stripped of your life! She picked up Hacinto from the ground and took him inside to take care of his wound. I felt satisfied, yet petrified of what my punishment would be.

I discerned that I was not Mother's favourite child. I was aware I looked ugly in comparison to my sisters and behaved differently from my siblings, but I was too young to understand whether the exclusion was due to my dark pigmentation, my skinny body, my almond-shaped eyes with double eyelids, or because I always operated at a hyper level.

The physical punishments inflicted by Mother escalated from isolation in the corner of our dining room in El Tigre, to whippings on my tiny legs with the black nylon belt I wore over my white school uniform in San Fernando.

Mother would hold me by the left arm and strike me until blotches swelled up on my legs like purple dragon tree leaves. My sisters would then tease me by singing in Spanish, *"¡Le florecieron!"* which meant, her flowers have blossomed.

This new type of punishment was psychologically tougher than the isolation in a dark corner because it left distinctive marks visible to everybody at home and at school. Not only was it physically painful, but it also produced emotional wounds that would bleed on my memory's walls for years to come.

The day I hit Hacinto, I remained alert, expecting Mother to come for me to draw more purple leaves on the back of my legs. Hours later when I had almost forgotten about it, Mother emerged from the kitchen carrying the black nylon belt. My sisters' murmurs alerted me. I jumped off the sofa where I was sitting in the family room and started running around the house. Mother ran after me. We were dashing about and squealing like two wild boars, from the bedroom to the kitchen and across the hall to the dining room.

The six-seater, rectangular, wooden table, covered with a colourfully embroidered, white tablecloth, occupied a big space in the middle of the dining room. I spun left and right around the table while Mother tried to catch me, again yelling, *"Enagsek ala oumrik!"* May you be stripped of your life! and *"Baddi edbahik!"* I will kill you!

After many revolutions around the table, I was about to get cornered. There was a slim opportunity for me to escape the clutches of my infuriated, abusive Mother, so without thinking of the consequences, I turned and punched the glass fascia of the dark wooden cupboard behind me with my little fist.

The punch was so robust, half the orderly placed glasses and ceramic dishes went cascading down and crashed on the polished concrete floor. Mother could not believe her eyes. Neither could I. I took advantage of the distraction and fled the dining room.

I sprinted across the backyard, scattering the hens and rooster pecking around the yard, until I reached the pond where our two pet ducks swam peacefully. I took a seat on the tarnished, old barrel turned on its side against the red block fence that separated our backyard from the outside world. The rusted barrel served as a hatching nest for the hens and sleeping room for the ducks. It took me several minutes to calm down as I gulped and gasped to catch my breath.

Distressed and apprehensive, I could not comprehend then that my aggressive and destructive behaviour, particularly toward

Mother, was an unconscious response to years of psychological abuse and physical punishment inflicted upon me.

I remained in the yard with the hens and ducks for hours. I contemplated what a fortunate life the poultry enjoyed, not having a mother who openly hated or mistreated them. I recalled then, one time three years earlier, when Mother almost killed me.

For mysterious reasons, there were days when Mother was so irritable and unapproachable, she could not even tolerate seeing me and my two younger sisters, Rasmille and Mima, playing around the house or making any noise. When we did, she would shout at us to stop. She also got easily infuriated and started big fights with Father.

That day, as I played with Rasmille and Mima in the bedroom behind the store, Mother shouted from the living room for us to stop the noise. I continued playing, ignoring Mother's demand. I did not hear her coming down the hall, but when she walked inside the bedroom, I saw the black nylon *chancleta*, sandal, she clutched in her hand and knew what that meant.

As I sat on the barrel reminiscing about that day, I could still feel the sting of the last slap from the chancleta on my back. She had chased me around the family room invoking the usual, wicked prayer *"Enagsek ala oumrik!"* May you be stripped of your life! and adding *"Inshallah bit mootee!"* I hope you die! It was difficult for her to run with one shoe on, so she paused and threw the chancleta down, slid her foot in it and started running after me again. When she got hold of me near the entrance to the kitchen, she threw me onto the floor and started kicking me.

"No! Stop!" I screamed. "I will not do it again!"

Thinking about that incident, it is possible that at that specific moment, Mother was reliving the events of the night her father found her hiding in the potato sack and kicked her until her ribs almost broke. Maybe her inability to face her father then and her repressed resentment were being channelled against me as a way of retribution. But even then, this behaviour could not be justifiable.

No matter the reason, lying on my right side on the floor, I was being kicked to death! Mother's foot, chancleta on, then landed on my fragile neck. I was choking under the heavy pressure of her foot.

"Mootee! Mootee!" Die! Die! she was shouting while I was gradually being choked.

I could feel the blood vessels on my forehead and temple begin to bulge. I thought I saw a black devil hovering above me as the chancleta kept me nailed to the floor. The more I resisted, the more I lost the capacity to breathe. I was immobilized under the weight of Mother's hatred. Today, as I recount this memory, I cannot help but think about the incident that happened to George Floyd in Minnesota in the summer of 2020, when the police officer knelt on his neck for 9 minutes and 29 seconds, until he suffocated. While the circumstances are different, the similarities are there, and the result could have been the same for me. But who in those days would have judged Mother?

The crowing of the rooster brought me back from the terrifying memory.

I looked around me and took a deep breath in relief, realizing I was still alone, surrounded by the poultry. I closed my eyes for a second and remembered how Father, alerted by the commotion, came to my rescue. He had come rushing from the store to find Mother choking me. He pushed her aside, reached down to pick me up in his arms, and placed me on the couch almost unconscious.

"How could you do such a thing?" I heard him yell.

As always, they ended up in a huge fight. Father retreated to the store, and Mother disappeared inside the kitchen, crying, while I laid on the sofa gathering my breath.

That was the first time Father saved me from Mother's infernal tentacles.

Giving Voice to My Silence

I stayed in the open-air shelter until the panic created by that awful memory faded, the sun plunged to the horizon, and the ducks went inside the barrel.

I then slowly walked back into the house and to the girls' bedroom, trying to avoid Mother, who by then calmed down, preparing dinner in the kitchen. I sank into the hammock hanging in the middle of the bedroom and fell asleep.

Montaha Hidefi

Chapter 3

I nearly jumped out of my seat at the voice of the captain who was making an announcement. A bit confused, still lethargic from the red-eye flight, I took off my eye mask. I could barely see around me in the dimly lit cabin. Michael was sipping a glass of wine, and he looked tired. I stretched myself up, reached to the window shade to my right, and raised it. The soft, bluish light of dawn above the clouds bathed my face. I smiled.

"Ladies and gentlemen, your captain speaking. We have started our descent..."

The dark blue colour of the ocean started appearing through the gaps in the thick clouds. The voice of the captain faded in the business-class cabin as I took out my iPhone to take pictures of our descent, as I always did.

As the aircraft descended, the clouds started clearing and I was able to capture the silver reflection of the early morning sun on the shoreline. It was magical!

What looked like an alien landscape started revealing itself. I could not stop shouting, "Wow! Wow!" while pressing the camera button. First, dark, lava rocks covered the terrain. Then, a volcanic crater appeared. In the distance, two enormous jets of steam were shooting into the air in front of a mountain range capped with snow. "Wow! Wow!" I kept saying. "Look at this! I love it!" Soon the ground turned into a dark, rusty desert. Then, dark lava rocks reappeared, this time covered with a blanket of yellowish, downy moss.

I felt as if we were landing on another planet. I was astonished. I had not anticipated the landscape to be so irregular, yet stunning. The closer we got to the airport, the more I had an incredible desire to stretch my arm out of the window and touch the soil with my bare hand. It was the most amazing landing experience I have ever had in my entire life. I was wide awake and felt I was the only person in the universe landing on the surface of an extraterrestrial land. I was happy.

As if that was not enough, as soon as we touched down, the first thing I saw on the tarmac was a purple Airbus A330 aircraft with three letters written on it in white. It read, WOW.

I wondered whether that was a coincidence or if the airport authorities knew passengers wowed on the way down, so they portrayed their experiences with this welcoming aircraft.

As our aircraft taxied toward the terminal, I started seeing more aircrafts with the same inscription. I understood then, this was an airline's name.

"Ladies and gentlemen, welcome to Reykjavik," announced the flight attendant. It was Monday, May 14, 2018.

This trip to Iceland was a gift from Michael to celebrate our 15 years of being together since we met online in 2003.

As the Icelandic Flybus left the airport building to take us to our hotel in the city, I was getting a better view of the landscape on my side of the highway. The road was still wet from the rain that had fallen the previous night. The Flybus was full of passengers from countless countries. To my left, Michael, who spent most the five-hour overnight flight awake sipping wine, was upset for my decision to book an economic transfer to the hotel with the public Flybus instead of a limousine. He wanted it to be our perfect vacation, away from other tourists.

The cacophony of Michael's complaints about my decision was getting annoying. However, as I concentrated on enjoying the view from my wide window, his voice started waning in the background as it collided with the memories that started emerging in my head.

The serpentine, wet, black surface of the highway looked like a snake slithering through the mossy, black volcanic rocks of the surrounding area. My mind was gliding on the wavy motion created by the swirling of the Flybus. I was transported back in time to 1972, the year when my father single-mindedly decided to return to his birth country, Syria. His decision precipitated our relocation at once. I was almost 13 at the time.

Because of the size of our family and the other paternal and maternal family members that came to Damascus to welcome our arrival, we were driven from there to Al-Kafr in two separate vehicles. Almost 45 minutes after we started the road trip, as we approached the first town on the road, an immense black mountain became visible on the horizon.

"This is Shahba, a historical city that saw the birth of Marcus Julius Philippus," Father said. "Roman emperor from 244 to 249, he was known as Philip the Arabian," he concluded.

Not only was the mountain black, but the surrounding area was immersed in an ocean of black volcanic boulders and rocks that rose from the ground in diverse formations with craters in between them and little or no vegetation. I had never experienced so much darkness before.

From there on, the colour of the landscape did not change. We got deeper into these enchanted, mountainous grounds as we approached our destination.

Five years later, while on board a Pullman bus on a solo trip from Al-Sweida to Damascus, I arrived at the same point near Shahba's mountain. I had to visit the head office of the government-owned shoe factory I had started to work at the previous year, at the age of 16.

When I got on the Pullman at Al-Sweida's out-of-town bus terminal, 20 minutes away from Shahba, there were no seats available except the aisle seat of the first row, behind the driver. A young man occupied the window seat. I took a seat next to him and kept to myself while the Pullman was getting ready to leave.

As soon as we left the terminal, the young man initiated an unsolicited chat with me. He asked my name and where I was from. I did not want to share information with him as I knew Syrian men could attempt to seduce young girls in any given occasion. He asked about the reason for my trip to Damascus. I respectfully told him I was going on a business trip, while trying to occupy myself with something inside my purse to show that I was busy and unable to talk to him.

Ten minutes down the road, as expected, he turned to me and said, "Do you know how beautiful you are?"

Without making eye contact I answered, "Thank you."

Shortly after, he was getting agitated. His legs were moving restlessly, and he changed position repeatedly. Though I was not looking at him, I could sense his eyes puncturing my skin like a knife. The seat had no armrest to divide us, so I felt his body temperature rising through his parka while his shoulder rubbed mine.

He unbuttoned his parka. With my peripheral vision, I noticed his right arm sinking inside the parka's front. His arm moved back and forth in a slow motion while pressing against mine. I supposed he was scratching his abdomen or leg. The friction against my arm and shoulder got stronger and the temperature of his arm through the parka mounted.

We were entering Shahba. I gradually turned my head toward the window to get a good look of the volcanic mountain I admired. He was looking at me. As we made eye contact, a shiver radiated from my head to my toes. I felt intimidated and uncomfortable.

With a big smile on his face, he winked as if signalling me to look down at him as he lifted the left side of his parka with the left hand inside his pocket. Unconsciously, my eyes turned in the direction he pointed at. His trousers were unzipped, and I saw the tip of his erection held in his right hand. He was masturbating on board the Pullman!

Trembling, my heart pounded faster than the Pullman's speed. My blood pressure rose. My temples swelled. I was at the verge of vomiting on his lap. I took a frantic, quick look at him and noticed his smile becoming larger.

Not knowing what to do, I wanted to stand up and run away. Tormented, I turned my head away and pushed my body as far away as possible from his to create a gap between our shoulders, arms, and legs. However, since the seat was not wide enough, I could still sense the heat emanating from his body.

Distressed, I looked around to ask for help. The closest person to me was the bus conductor, who was sitting on the seat of the same row across the aisle, gazing out the window. I looked behind me. Most passengers were sleeping, and nobody was paying attention to the front of the bus.

In a desperate attempt to put an end to the situation, I reached out to the conductor. With a simulated smile, I asked him if he would not mind trading seats with me. I was not expecting he would accept with no hesitation and without even asking me why I wanted to trade seats. I never got to know who he was, but I have never forgotten his act of kindness.

As I stood up to exchange seats, everything around me turned in circles. My entire body vibrated. I was falling into an abyss. I dragged myself to the conductor's seat and allowed my numbed body to drop onto it.

I looked out the window and took many deep breaths. Scared, I wondered if I should tell the conductor. Should I ask the driver to pull over, so I could get out to vomit or catch another ride to Damascus? I did not know the answers. But that was not the first nor the last time I experienced such blatant and unwanted sexual touching in public.

Montaha Hidefi

Chapter 4

Swallowing my uncertainties in silence as the Pullman continued its trajectory, I contemplated the volcanic rocks that decorated the topography of the deserted lands ahead of Damascus, where the Syrian Armed Forces had military airports, and I recalled in dismay the first time I saw an adult male's genitals.

In San Fernando, Sundays were traditionally considered a family day. Every Sunday, Father took us for a *paseo*, an excursion, for the family to get out, stop at a *bomba* for gas and refrescos, and spend time together. I loved the paseos as they provided the opportunity to leave the house and explore something different with my sisters and drink refrescos in the scorching hot weather.

Due to the size of our family, the adults had devised the sitting-in-the-car chart to avoid fights among us. Father, whose cauchos business had flourished, had recently replaced his old, green Chevy with a light-grey Dodge. He and Mother occupied the front seats. My little brother, Nabil, who was born five years after Hacinto, sat on Mother's lap. Danela occupied the rear left seat, behind Father, while Yusra occupied the rear right seat, behind Mother. I sat next to Danela, Rasmille next to Yusra, and Mima and Hacinto in the middle.

San Fernando's working class received their paycheque on Fridays. To many, that triggered an all-night party, drinking *aguardiente de caña*, a popular alcoholic brew distilled from sugar cane and considered the local beer. Men would drink aguardiente until they got drunk or until they spent all the money earned from the working week. Certain men got intoxicated for many days and would remain in the streets, wandering around shouting vulgar words at pedestrians or drivers.

On one occasion, around 1967, as the sun started its descent to the horizon, Father was circling the public square on our way back home from the paseo. Through the first shadows of dusk, I spotted a drunk man stumbling at the top of the three steps around the square. He was chubby, and his right arm hung down the side of his imbalanced body, carrying a bottle of aguardiente.

As the car approached him, the last rays of light revealed more of his figure. His left hand was holding onto something just below his waistline. It looked like a big, black, fluffy *platano* poking through the zipper of his filthy khakis. He was swaying the swollen platano up and down with his hand while shouting "*carajo, puta*" and other obscene words that I had never heard before. When I got older, I realized the drunk man was saying "fucking whore."

Danela and I had the best visual angle of the scene.

"*¡O mírale la pipa!*" Danela shouted out while laughing. Oh, look at his dick!

"*Ghamdou younkun!*" Mother yelled. Cover your eyes!

"*Yal'an hal balad!*" Father mumbled under his breath. Damn this country!

While I had heard the word pipa before, I had never seen nor imagined how it looked. At the age of seven, it was the first sexual object to which I had been exposed. While I could not fathom the meaning or importance of this scene, I knew by the fact that my parents and eldest sister were troubled and concerned by it that I must have witnessed a prohibited act. This incident was never mentioned at home, ever. It was suppressed and left there where it happened, as it ended with the onward movement of the vehicle.

That explicit act, to which I had been accidentally subjected, stayed in my mind. I could not erase the image from my memory bank. Even in my adulthood, whenever I encountered a man, the first thing that came to my mind was the image of that inebriated man exposing his genitalia in a public square, which was alarming and left me feeling uncomfortable and nervous. I never understood whether it was the ridiculousness of that occurrence that marked me or the gravity of it that scarred my child's psyche.

My eyes flickered as I brought my mind back to what had just happened on the Pullman bus. The remainder of the

Giving Voice to My Silence

journey to Damascus seemed to take forever that day. The belief that there must be something in all men that made them like to expose themselves would not leave my mind.

Just before we arrived in Damascus, I began speculating what would happen when we reached the out-of-town bus terminal. Would this offensive individual be stalking me? How was I supposed to react if he did?

I was the first passenger to step out of the Pullman after it stopped. I rushed out of the terminal, stopped at the sidewalk of the busy street, and hailed a taxi. I was still in shock. My heart was still pounding like a pair of drums invoking the spirits of our ancestors to bring rain to help me wash away the creepy sensations of anxiety and disgust.

Getting a vacant taxi to stop at the terminal in Damascus was in general difficult. But that day, the summoned spirits of our ancestors heard the call. A taxi stopped shortly after I started hailing. I opened the door, got in, and asked the driver to take me to my destination. I was finally in a safer place and hoped to disappear on the crowded streets of the capital, until I heard the driver asking, *"Min wein hazertık?"* Where are you from?

Montaha Hidefi

Chapter 5

The streets of Damascus and the taxi drivers were anything but safe for a teenager like me in the 1970s. Coming of age in Syria, a country with a rich culture and art history but holding to traditional values that seemed archaic in contrast to my birth country's liberal morals, I grew tiresome figuring out how to fit in and, as a female, how to be treated with dignity and respect.

Whenever I walked the streets of Damascus or had a taxi ride while on my own, I came to realize that the typical Syrian male felt he had an intrinsic right to seduce, grab, grope, or kiss me, or any other female. I was subjected to never-ending groping and touching from men walking down the streets and continual innuendos and offensive invitations from male drivers.

In the second half of the 1980s, I lived in Damascus while attending university for my bachelor's degree in French literature and master's in translation. During that time, I became aware that two of the reasons I was considered easy prey were my accent and dialect.

I learned to speak Arabic after our relocation to Syria. It took me two years to be able to make grammatically correct, coherent sentences. Yet I was never able to drop my Latin American accent. Although *Castellano*, Castilian, the formal spoken Spanish in Venezuela, has Arabic influences, the influences are fundamentally lexical. When it comes to articulation, Spanish is liquid and nasal while Arabic is particularly rich in guttural sounds. These differences impacted the way I spoke Arabic.

The combination of my foreign accent with the southern dialect of Al-Sweida made it easy to detect I was an *ajnabiyah,* foreigner. Foreign women were considered approachable and expected to welcome sexual innuendos and even have sexual relationships with anyone. I never understood the background of that preconceived notion, but I did endure its overwhelming outcome for as long as I lived in Syria.

One early morning of 1985, I grabbed a taxi from Rukun Eldin, a neighbourhood in the northeast of Damascus where I rented a room. I was going to the out-of-town bus terminal to travel to Al-Sweida for the weekend. After I told the driver where to take me, he asked where I was from, a question I heard from every taxi driver.

Although I knew he would not believe me, I answered my usual, "I am from here."

He repeated, *"Min wein hazertik?"* Where are you from? I answered again, *"Min hoon!"* From here!

"Mo ma'oul!" he said. It is not possible!

The continuous, unsolicited harassment from taxi drivers stimulated me to improvise techniques to stop them from bothering me. As I interacted with Damascenes more often, I was able to express myself in their dialect, while still maintaining the foreign accent.

I took a deep breath, thinking "Here we go again!"

"Heza min eradat Allah. Enta mo mou'min? Ma bte'bal mashe'at Allah?" I asked in a Damascene, foreign accent. This is Allah's will! Aren't you a devotee? Are you contradicting Allah's will?

He looked at me through the rear-view mirror with massive eyes, not expecting such a response. His eyebrows almost touched his hairline. I knew I was hitting on a sensitive chord because no Muslim Damascene would mess around with Allah. I was so proud of myself for using that tactic.

"Mashallah!" he apologized. As Allah wills! Then he stopped talking.

I stifled a giggle. I was happy to be left in peace for the rest of the ride to the terminal.

It slowly began to dawn on me how I had turned a situation around simply by being assertive and either playing on a man's sense of decency or by invoking Allah's name, or even a female relative like his mother or sister. It was a survival mechanism, given the circumstances.

Chapter 6

A year later, in the scorching summer of 1986, I hailed a taxi early one afternoon at one of Damascus's roundabouts. To support my graduation year, I had a part-time job as a typewriter instructor at an office that provided services to university students. The office closed at two o'clock for lunch break, and I had to leave.

When I first started to recollect the details of the disgraceful and humiliating incident that will unfold in the following pages, I realized I had buried the memory of it so deep in the abyss of my past, I could not remember with clarity all the details. At the suggestion of my Chilean friend Ruth, who knew about the incident when it happened, I decided to seek the services of a hypnotherapist to unblock the events of that day.

The hypnotherapist recommended that I contact an age regression therapist. She said there was only one of them in the Guelph area in Ontario, Shelley Timoffee. I phoned Shelley and got an appointment.

Age regression is a guided meditation that allows the individual to access memories from our current life's past. Memories "that we may have tucked away for safekeeping," according to Shelley's website, www.soulsease.com.

My appointment was for Monday, March 12, 2018. I went to see Shelley with no expectations. I had read various books about past-life regression and understood that it was about retrieving information from a previous life that might be relevant to one's current life and might help in making peace with oneself. I was, however, unfamiliar with age regression and felt reluctant, but my desire to write the details of this incident surpassed my hesitation.

Shelley put me in a profoundly relaxed state of mind and guided me with her voice to embark on a journey to the centre of my deepest inner universe with the objective of finding a key that would unfasten the repressed memory.

For over an hour, I went through a colossal, emotional roller coaster. From being calm to being frantic, I crossed the darkness of my inner universe to find a beautiful golden sand beach from where, minutes later, I was catapulted to the day when the appalling incident took place. During the inner journey, I experienced a multitude of emotions; I cried, I laughed, I was angry, I was scared, I felt hatred and even physical pain in my left arm. I was shivering throughout the session even though I was covered by a thick blanket. However, it was all worth the outcome. I was able to crack the code and access the details of what I had been exposed to that day.

Shelley recorded the session for me to listen to later when I felt in a mental disposition to do so. It took over three months before I felt ready to listen to the recording and transcribe the details. This incident had affected me so much, I was running away from it.

Roundabouts in Damascus were jammed in the early afternoons. Traffic flowed in a systematic, though chaotic, manner through lanes not demarcated by road paint, but created by the stream of vehicles. During the session, I remembered walking around the square, waving for over half an hour, to no avail. Taxis would not stop! I was in despair. It occurred to me to cross the six lanes, making my way through heavy traffic, and blowing horns to stand at the inner side of the roundabout, with my arm stuck out, hailing as if I were a traffic police officer. I could no longer see the statue erected at the centre of the roundabout as I faced the endless river of vehicles revolving counter-clockwise around the square in a pilgrimage formation.

During the age regression session, as I saw myself undertaking this dangerous risk, I thought I had been fortunate to not have been run over.

After a short while, almost deaf from the loud roaring engines and blaring horns, I spotted a vacant taxi in the lane adjacent to me. "Taxi, taxi!" I waved and shouted to be heard in the commotion.

I had a quick eye contact with the driver. He slowed down, trying not to stop, as the circulation was unforgiving.

Giving Voice to My Silence

I opened the passenger door behind the driver while the vehicle was still in motion. A strong cloud of cigarette stink mixed with stagnant, sour sweat almost knocked me out as I was getting in. The black, faux leather of the distressed, back seat had a big crack showing the once white fibre of the lining. I hesitated for a moment but pushed myself in as the driver yelled, *"Yalla, yalla!"* Come on, come on! It was a miracle I managed it in one piece.

I rolled down the window to get rid of the repulsive odour as it was difficult to breathe, but the warm breeze coming through was diffusing the odour in the air of the vehicle instead of letting it get out. Still, I left the window half rolled down to allow the air to flow.

I told the driver, who was adjusting the rear-view mirror with his right hand, to take me to the university dorms located in Mazzeh. I was sharing a room there with Ruth and another student, also from Chile.

The driver nodded. In the mirror, I could see his eyes fixated on me. He must have been in his late twenties, early thirties. I could not see his entire face, only his eyes.

"Min wein hazertik?" he started. Where are you from?

To calm myself down and prevent additional, typical questions, I did not answer and focused my gaze outside the window. I let my eyes and mind wander in the void of that chaotic afternoon, scrolling behind the glass of the half-open window at the pedestrians, the transit, the people hailing taxis, and the residential buildings in the background.

I suddenly realized that we had passed my destination. *"La wein rayeh?"* I asked. Where are you going?

"We are going to take a small tour around," he replied.

"Why?" I asked, feeling a bit nervous.

"I want to show you the city," he replied.

"Why would you want to show me the city? I live here," I said. "Please take me to my destination."

Ignoring my request, he continued uphill through the traffic. I recognized the neighbourhoods and knew that shortly after, there would be fewer vehicles on the street and no buildings. We would be isolated.

I began thinking of a plan to leave. I pressed my legs so tight together, I could almost hear the clacking of my knee bones against each other. Yet I knew I had to maintain a relaxed position and show no fear.

The traffic was getting lighter as the vehicle climbed the streets toward Jebel Qasioun, the mountain overlooking the city of Damascus. The beautiful panoramic vistas of the city from the top of Qasioun were known as one of the main attractions for family evening getaways where people could grab an orange juice or a black tea from one of the tin stands opened at night, while enjoying the lights of the big city.

Qasioun was also known for attracting dating couples for romantic indulgences, secluded from the city while still easily accessible.

Very few people ascended Qasioun during daytime. If they did, it was to engage in flirtations or romance away from the view of others since it was forbidden to show public affection.

The beautiful scenery of the city started appearing through the right window as the vehicle was getting closer to the parking lot on the top of Qasioun. I was hoping to see other vehicles to ensure safety. I was sure the driver would not initiate any advances if there were other vehicles and people up there.

My heart plummeted as I realized there was nobody else. He slowed down, made a right half-turn, and stopped the vehicle at the cliff.

As soon as he stopped, I opened the door and got out of the vehicle. I knew no matter what happened, being in the open was a better option than being trapped inside the vehicle. I walked around pretending to enjoy the panoramic view as I tried to get as far away from him as possible. He opened the door and stepped out. I looked at him to anticipate his next move.

"What is your name?" he asked.

"Maria," I replied spontaneously. I always used Maria when I did not want to disclose my identity.

"Where are you from?" he continued, walking toward me.

"From here," I replied.

I was getting more nervous. I was all alone with this individual in this immense open space. From his expression, I knew his intent was to have a private moment with me. Whether it was a kiss, a touch, or sex, whatever he could get me doing, would be considered a great achievement for him.

"Why did you bring me here?" I asked. "What do you want from me? Could you please take me back?"

"Why are you in such a hurry?" he asked. "Look! We are alone. We could have some fun."

Not having a plan and to distract him, I asked, "Do you have sisters?"

"Yes. I have two sisters," he said.

"Where do you live?" I continued, an attempt to delay anything he had in mind while hoping that another vehicle would show up.

"I live in Bab Touma," he replied, referring to a Christian neighbourhood in Damascus.

"Would you like your sisters to be in this situation?" I asked. "Would you like them to be brought up here by an unknown taxi driver?"

Oblivious to my anxiety, he asked, "Why are you talking about my sisters?"

"Because I have sisters too," I said. "I also have brothers. They wouldn't like me to be here with a stranger."

"We are just having fun," he insisted.

"I don't think it's fun!" I replied. "I want to go to the dorms to prepare for my class."

"It won't take too long. I just want to have some fun with you," he pressed.

I was unsure which was making me perspire more, the fear of being raped on the top of Qasioun or the red shirt I was wearing under the burning sun, but I was pleading to the universe for a miracle.

I kept looking at the city to hide my anxiety while the sweat was building up on my upper lip. Suddenly, I heard a sound in the distance. It seemed like an engine! I turned to my right, where he was standing near me. Behind him, I saw a white Toyota Land Cruiser approaching.

I sighed. I recognized it was a Mukhabarat's vehicle, the Military Intelligence Service of Syria. Controlled by the president's office, the Mukhabarat were very influential. They were known to be ruthless and acted either explicitly or undercover. People feared them. Although their vehicles were unmarked, everybody recognized them.

The Mukhabarat's vehicle stopped twenty metres away from us. The front doors opened and two men with intimidating demeanours briskly stepped out and hurried toward us.

Aware of the dangerous situation I was in, I collected myself, forced my right foot in front of the left one and began walking toward them with my head up.

I said in a humble tone, "Could you please help me?"

"What is happening?" asked one of them, while the other was scanning the area.

"I asked to be taken to the university dorms and he brought me here instead," I said.

They stopped for a second and looked at me in silence. Then, as if ignoring me, they continued toward the taxi driver. I stood watching them in terror. I was wondering whether I was about to become the subject of a gang rape or if they were going to push him down the cliff and then rape me themselves.

They initiated a private talk with the taxi driver, which I was unable to hear. I looked in the other direction, trying to find an escape route in case they all turned against me. The Mukhabarat were not trustworthy, and it was possible that the worst could happen.

Giving Voice to My Silence

A moment later, they walked back in my direction while the driver was getting into the taxi. They told me to get in the taxi. I said, "No!"

"He will take you to the dorms," one of them said. "We will be behind you. He cannot do anything to you. Go!"

I walked slowly to the taxi, opened the back door behind the front passenger seat and slowly got in. I looked at the driver. His face was red. I presumed they smacked him, and if they did not, I thought, they would do so after he dropped me off.

He started the engine, put the vehicle in reverse, and left the parking lot. As he started descending Qasioun, I looked through the rear windshield and saw the Mukhabarat's vehicle following us.

Still frightened, I took a deep breath, pressed my knees together, and for the first time grasped the meaning of the common saying: "The enemy of my enemy is my friend."

As he drove downhill, I stayed alert in anticipation of any unexpected reaction. I knew that if the Mukhabarat's vehicle was following us, I was safe.

He looked at me in the rear-view mirror and said, "I am sorry. I only wanted to have some fun with you."

"Ana mo sharmouta!" I said. I am not a prostitute!

"I am sorry! I have sisters too and wouldn't want them to be treated this way," he added.

When we reached the gated university dorms, I pulled a 10 Syrian pound bill out of my purse, double what the fare would have been, and threw it on the front seat, opened the door, and got out quickly. The Mukhabarat individuals nodded to me from their vehicle.

A large group of students stood in front of the entrance gate to the dorms. Stripped of my dignity and unable to understand how I escaped being raped, I leaned against the four-metre-high concrete fence to compose myself. I felt exhausted, empty, and degraded. I took a deep breath. I pulled my student identity card from my purse and stood in line to show it to the military guards armed with machine guns.

To walk from the gate to my room took around 10 minutes. As I stumbled along, tired, and weary, I wanted to have a cigarette. I saw a brown bench shining under the sun, so I decided to have a moment to myself before getting to the room. I sat and went to light up a cigarette but remembered it was not allowed for females to smoke in public at the dorms.

I stood up and continued walking. None of my roommates were home. I slid the aluminum-framed window open, lit up a cigarette, and sat at the edge of my bed.

Five minutes later, the door of the room opened, and Ruth came in.

"Qué pasa?" she asked. What is going on?

Between tears, sighs, and laments, I told her the story. She held me and exclaimed, "You are so strong!" She continued hugging me. I did not fathom why she thought I was strong. "How did you do that? How did it occur to you to ask for help from the bad guys to deal with a bad guy?" Ruth recognized that the Mukhabarat could have taken me somewhere instead of helping me, but I had been brave and took a chance.

I laid back on the bed while she prepared a cup of coffee. As I reran the details in my mind, I realized I had exuded power by trusting the Mukhabarat, but I thought the strength I displayed on Qasioun was only a disguise, a cry for help. Living in a country where I always had to keep my defences up was wearing me down as a person and breaking me as a female. I needed to leave the country to free myself from that hell on Earth.

Chapter 7

Thirty-two years and countless cities around the world later, before leaving my in-laws' house in the countryside of Bahama, North Carolina, I turned on the outdoor lights to make sure we had enough illumination at the front entrance.

We had spent that day, June 9, 2018, celebrating my father-in-law, Siegfried's, 90th birthday. Between Michael, his brother Paul and wife, Julie, his cousin Eric, and me, we pulled together an enjoyable family-only party that left Siegfried weeping with joy as he blew out the candles on his cake.

"No one has ever done anything like this for me before!" he claimed.

It was around 10 in the evening when we left. I was carrying a bag with two wine bottles, my laptop, my iPad, and some other trivial things to take back to the inn. I opened the front door to get to the rental vehicle parked in the driveway.

Although I had all the lights turned on, it was quite dark outside the limits of the old, white wooden fence surrounding the porch. My mother-in-law, Eva, had spent part of the afternoon contemplating the surrounding greenery as she rested with Siegfried on an outdoor loveseat placed across the porch, while we were setting up and cooking for the gathering. The loveseat was somehow obstructing the shortcut between the door and the flight of stairs leading to the driveway. I needed to get around it to reach the stairs.

After taking a couple of steps around the loveseat, the vigorous black Labrador, who spent the day locked inside Paul and Julie's adjacent house, bounced up the flight of stairs in my direction.

Surprised and frightened, I jumped back to prevent a collision. My slick, leather sandals destabilized me. Instead of taking a step back, I slipped and landed on the porch's wooden floor, taking a great hit on my buttocks. Eric, who was two feet behind me, hurried to my rescue.

"Get it away from me!" I yelled; afraid the dog would jump on me.

Eric managed to haul the dog away.

The crash was so loud, everybody hurried out to find me still on the floor.

I had so much pain in my low back and tailbone, I was unsure I would be able to stand up. I expected Michael or anyone else to lend me a hand, but instead, I heard voices muttering, "It is only a dog! It will not do anything," the usual reaction of individuals dealing with people like me who are afraid of dogs.

The 50 seconds or so I spent sitting on my rear felt more like 50 agonizing years. I was catapulted back to the late 1960s and into the dark kitchenette of our house in San Fernando.

Since our house was an old church converted into a dwelling, the property owner had built two partitions in the corner of the open space, right before the bedroom, to serve as a kitchenette. The big, open space served as sitting room and porch overlooking the 900-square-metre backyard. A metre-high cement fence separated the backyard from the open space. Eventually, my sister Yusra and I had the fence capped with our cultivated portulacas, coleus, elephant ears, Moses in the cradle, and other colourful foliage. Since the kitchenette had no actual door, Mother stitched a flimsy curtain with a green, floral print and nailed it to the walls to cover the entrance.

The kitchenette was small and had no windows, so it was dark, even during daytime. I always had the chills whenever I was asked to fetch something from it, so I frequently protested, saying I was scared.

Mother used my fear of the kitchenette's darkness as punishment. Whenever I disobeyed her commands or defied her, she shouted, *"¡Te mando a la cocina para que te coma el perro negro!"* I will send you to the kitchen and let the black dog eat you!

The first time Mother told me that, I was too young and did not comprehend the meaning of that menacing statement.

Afterward, when I disobeyed her, she grabbed my arm, dragged me through the sitting room, chucked me inside the kitchenette, and shouted the same threat about the black dog: *"Khalle'el kalb el-asswad yakleek!"* Let the black dog eat you!

Tossed on the floor like spillage, I was horrified. I cried and asked for forgiveness. "No! No! I will not do it again!"

As she walked away, I curled up in the fetal position and sheltered my face with my hands since I did not know from what angle, through the darkness, the black dog would attack. My muscles tensed. The shadows of blackness spread all over my skin like thorny, evil feathers. My heart was pounding so loud, the booms filled the kitchenette. I started seeing big, fiery red circles and felt long canine teeth plunge into my arms and legs. I pressed my eyelids with all the strength I had left to stop the chilling images. I was unable to determine whether they were drawn by my fertile imagination or if I were actively being devoured by a black dog.

I could not tell how long I was left alone there, but it was one of the longest nightmares I had in my childhood. I heard Mother walk back in. She pulled me up by my arm, dragged me back to the sitting room, and dumped me on the couch like a piece of garbage. "I hope you learned your lesson!"

Affirmative. I had learned a lesson beyond anything she could have imagined. I have been terrified of dogs ever since.

As the threats with the black dog continued, I was careful not to upset Mother to a degree that she would toss me back into the dog's pit. My survival instinct and the fear of the black dog powered my creativity and I conceived methods to evade the punishment, which included not telling her the truth and doing things behind her back. And so, I learned to hide everything from her to save my skin.

Nowadays, even though I know the root cause of my fear of dogs, and despite numerous phobia therapies I have subjected myself to with the aim of getting over it, the terror of being eaten or beaten by a black dog in the darkness has been a lifelong fear.

Regardless of the time of day I see a dog being walked on the street, I change sides and do my best to avoid visual or physical contact with any dog.

Chapter 8

The fear of darkness started much earlier in my childhood.

Even before the age of four, I was an agile girl. I behaved in ways that upset Mother and constantly asked questions she was unable to answer. I was seeking her support to nurture my curiosity to discover the world, to no avail.

Whenever I misbehaved or disobeyed an order to remain quiet, Mother would snarl, *"Enagsek ala oumrik!"* May you be stripped of your life! Sometimes *"Inshallah bit mootee!"* I hope you die! or *"Allah you-hurkek!"* May Allah burn you! While I did not speak Arabic at the time, I recognized that Mother was praying for evil things to happen.

Since Mother's malevolent prayers did not result in any sweltering or death, I started doubting her wicked invocations. Consequently, the frequency of my disobedient acts increased as if to evaluate her honesty. By then, what in current times would be classified as depression had progressed for Mother, and she was unable to cope with the disturbances resulting from my misbehaviour, so she had to improvise ways to tame me. She resorted to physical punishment.

Whenever she deemed it necessary, she ordered me to get down on my knees and face the dark corner of the windowless dining room of our house in El Tigre. The length of the time-out depended on the trouble I caused and Mother's irritation level. Sometimes it lasted for 10 minutes, and often it continued for as long as half an hour, or more, when she forgot that I was being punished. During the time-out, I was not allowed to stand up, rest on my heels, or communicate with any of my sisters.

I was my parents' third daughter, the first to be born in Venezuela, on January 4, 1960. It was exactly 9 months and 15 days after Mother's arrival to El Tigre, following a month-long transoceanic voyage aboard a Turkish ocean liner that departed from the Port of Beirut in Lebanon, via Genoa, Italy, and arrived at La Guaira Port of Venezuela in April of 1959.

Father was 32, while Mother was around 26. Nobody knew her exact birth date because there were no records of it, and she never ever celebrated a birthday.

Mother recounts that I was born with a dark blue, almost purple, skin colour, which was in stark contrast with my family's fair pigmentation. This might have been the main reason they nicknamed me Negra.

As a baby, I represented a challenge. I cried incessantly when I was left to rest in my *cuna*, cradle. The only way I would stop crying and fall asleep was by being rocked in the arms of my sisters, Danela, and Yusra. Nobody knew the reason for my discomfort, but I grew up seeking comfort and affection.

Years later, Danela revealed to me something that made the fine hair on my entire body spike like needles. To make me stop crying, she and Yusra fetched white crab spiders from the porch, attached their silky string to one of their fingers, and wound them down to my face like a yo-yo. However, Danela added that even that improvisation did not stop my crying. When she told me this, I could not wrap my head around such a cruel act inflicted on a baby. No wonder I grew up terrified of spiders and still am to this day.

It was during the moments of seclusion in the corner that I developed a horrifying fear of darkness. To evade the shadows forming before me, I would close my eyes tightly and clench my teeth. My imagination, nevertheless, would continue to conjure up creepy images that sometimes took the shape of a giant, long-legged, deep brown, hairy spider crawling down the wall facing me, so I would tighten my eyes even more and my mouth would dry up like an arid desert. The crawling spider would then mutate into a threatening, demonic red figure with long horns soaring above my head, causing the hair on the back of my neck to prickle like painful thorns, my heart to race, and my upper lip to bead with sweat.

These moments of mental horror and physical cruelty were to persist in my mind for as long as I lived. They augmented my phobia of spiders and were at the origin of my disbelief in God and my hatred toward Mother, three major pillars that carved my essence and shaped the core of my personality, not only as a female, but also as a human being.

How could I have believed in Allah, the God of the Druze that Mother invoked to burn me and kill me but that luckily did not answer?

At the age of four, it was impossible for me to know anything about my family's religion since the Druze community maintains the details of their faith in total secrecy because other religious communities have violently persecuted them for centuries. Druzism is a monotheistic religion whose adherents live primarily in Syria, Lebanon, Jordan, and Israel, with small migrant communities around the world.

I determined at such a tender age that God was a Druze punishment tool Mother used to scare me. I started believing that God was an enormous, despicable spider whose web was in the darkest upper corner of our dining room, and I hated it.

At an early age I was well-acquainted with Mother's unscrupulous disciplinary tactics, the physical and mental abuse, but I was never able to block out the phantoms created by my imagination during these "go-to-the-corner," solitary corrective sessions.

When I was not being corrected, I was fond of sketching things that helped me forget the imaginary creatures that terrified me. I drew colourful flowers and green trees, but even that irritated Mother who wanted me to sit and remain silent.

I fantasized having a painter's brush to transform the wings of darkness of the world around me, to paint them with happy colours: red, yellow, green, and blue. But Mother censured even fantasies. It was as if she could read my mind.

My sisters and I grew up being told not to smile or laugh when Father was at home. We were to remain in total silence, which was punishment. Inevitably, when asked to be silent, we would burst into laughter as we looked at each other, again drawing Mother's wrath.

In contrast, Father, a reserved man who did not smoke, never drank alcohol, and believed in God, was tender but mostly serious and composed. As was typical of the era, he spent most his time at work, did not participate in the child-rearing, and was not aware of Mother's discipline style or her moralizing methods of raising us. While he was not known for displaying any sign of affection, whether in public or privately, when he was at home, he would sit in one of the white, synthetic leather armchairs on the front porch of the house, and I would perch on the wooden arm of the chair while he played with me. I loved those moments of tenderness, and they remain the most vivid memories I have of Father during my childhood.

Life in El Tigre was not all roses for my parents in the 1960s. Father had a day job as a carpenter, earning 50 Venezuelan bolivars per week, the equivalent of US$15 at that time. With so many mouths to feed and a house to take care of, my parents were living in utter poverty. To hold their socks up around their calves, Yusra and Danela had to tie them with elastic ribbons. As they grew, their clothes were passed down to me. Our diet was limited to the bare necessities, and we did not have a social life outside of the Syrian community and our neighbours.

These harsh conditions, as well as the distance separating my parents from their home country, *Al-bilad* as they called it, and being unable to write, read, or even have a telephone, draped Mother in emotional isolation. When recalling that period, she recounts that she was slowly being drawn into a black hole of solitude and desperation.

As if that was not enough, one night Danela went to bed with a high fever. When she woke up next morning she could not feel or move her legs. She was paralyzed from the waist down. The doctor who came to check on her announced that she was hit by poliomyelitis (polio) and that she needed immediate care at the orthopaedic hospital in the capital, Caracas, around 450 kilometres from El Tigre, a trip that took around six hours by car.

Father transported Danela to Caracas the next day, leaving Mother behind to look after us. Danela was immediately hospitalized and remained at the hospital for over a year. One in 200 polio cases led to irreversible paralysis, and since polio had no cure, it was unknown whether Danela would survive or walk ever again.

Fortunately, with the determination of Father, who visited Danela often and encouraged her to walk, she was able to regain mobility.

Whenever Mother evoked these days, she said those were agonizing times for her as her first-born laid at a distant hospital and she was unable to see her, talk to her, or even know her condition. She felt cursed to live a life of anguish and poverty. This was not the life she was expecting in a new world full of hope. This was not the Venezuelan promise.

The news about my grandfather's death also fuelled Mother's sadness. She would sit for long hours in the dark dining room lamenting the obscurity of her life and crying. She wandered around the house barefoot, almost hovering weightless like a ghost. She lost the ability to meet our basic needs for love and affection. She became bitter and often violent toward me as she still considered me a challenge. I was different from my siblings, not only in complexion, but also in personality.

I was too young to understand Mother's state of mind, but whatever she was going through was affecting us as a family and me as a child. I was growing faster than my age, and in self-preservation, I needed to learn how to recognize the warning signs and how to escape her wrath, which, of course, only angered her more. I wanted to feel loved by the person that was my mother but did not know how to behave to deserve her love and attention.

Although Danela survived the polio infection, she remained disabled and limped her entire life. But her disability did not prevent her from being a bright woman with superior handcraft skills. At 15, she was a tailor and hairdresser. She created sewing patterns and sewed all our outfits. Her knitting, crocheting, and embroidery work were spectacular and contributed to her earnings. She lived in Syria, married, and had four children. At the age of 52, she had a cerebral infarction that left the left side of her body paralyzed. Four years later, in August of 2010, Mother, who was looking after her at the time, left her room for fresh air. On her return minutes later, she found Danela had died alone.

The news of Danela's passing was gut-wrenching. She was not only my sister and friend, but I also considered her the mother I longed for. The distance separating us and the long 17 years since 1993 when we last saw each other in person meant that I did not have the opportunity to say a proper goodbye.

Chapter 9

After my father-in-law's birthday celebration, Michael and I had planned a three-day stopover in Chicago, Illinois, so I could attend the 50th edition of Neocon 2018, an annual furniture trade show I had attended since 2010.

We arrived in Chicago on Monday, June 11. I spent Tuesday at the Merchandise Mart, where the show would take place, and met with friends and fellow members of the Color Marketing Group, who, like me, were attending the show seeking trends and colour inspiration.

On Wednesday, I left the Mart around three in the afternoon and decided to walk to my hotel instead of taking a taxi. The weather was beautiful. The sun was shining and there was almost no wind, which is unusual for Chicago.

I wanted to enjoy a stroll and take photos of buildings along the way, as a follow-up to the Chicago Architecture Foundation's River Cruise Michael and I took earlier that day.

The hotel was on Michigan Avenue, in the heart of the Magnificent Mile. I stopped to take a photo every time a building grabbed my attention. As tourists filled the streets and the circulation of the early afternoon was heavy, I felt invisible. Everyone was minding their own business. No one paid attention to me. Recollections of times past, packed with appalling, unsolicited street experiences, flooded my present.

I remembered that day in April of 1997 when Travel Options in Montreal, Quebec, called to let me know I could pick up my ticket to Dubai in the United Arab Emirates. I had attended classes for two years, on evenings and weekends, and was to complete my post-graduate studies in business administration at the University of Sherbrooke in Longueuil, on the South Shore of Montreal, on April 16. I had booked my flight for the 18th, two days after my final exam.

At the time, I was employed at a branch of a privately held American agency providing professional services to VIP job seekers who earned over CAN$100,000 per year. Although the office was in the affluent suburb of Westmount in Montreal, it was a temporary job, and I had no employment security or development plan. The owner, an older Jewish gentleman, was about to retire and needed the services of an assistant to prepare material to mail out and organize monthly networking meetings for the members.

My objective in graduating from a Canadian university was to improve my career prospects and get permanent employment where I could earn an income consistent with my recent Canadian post-graduate status.

My friend Mahmoud, who lived in Doha, Qatar, and whom I had not seen for 10 years, had asked me the previous winter to meet him in Dubai. I could not afford the $1,893 ticket to Dubai with my weekly $700 income that served to pay for my studies, rent, and utility bills. I lived on the bare minimum, spending below $50 per week on food and personal expenses. So, I decided not to entertain the offer to travel to Dubai, until Patrick, one of the owners and manager of another company that was headquartered on the same floor of the agency I worked at, offered to lend me $1,000 to help buy the ticket. I was reluctant to accept; however, Patrick insisted I must take the opportunity and travel to Dubai.

I did not think at the time that Patrick's generosity would influence my life and turn it around 180 degrees. When I learned that he passed from a heart attack in June of 2015, I was saddened, and I was never able to thank him properly for his act of kindness.

The Emirates Airlines plane landed in Dubai in the early morning of April 21, 1997, with a day's delay. I had originally booked my flight with KLM, but an unexpected snowstorm in Montreal on that day delayed my flight. On arrival in Amsterdam, I had missed my connecting flight to Dubai, so I was redirected via London on Emirates.

As I stepped out of the aircraft, the boiling, humid air of Dubai smacked me in the face. I had not experienced anything like it before.

Giving Voice to My Silence

The glow of the sun reflecting on the tarmac was so extraordinary, it blinded me. I slowly descended the mobile staircase. When I reached the last step, I pointed my camera at the airport building and snapped a picture. The two military police officers standing at each side of the staircase shouted at me, "No photo! No photo!" I immediately concealed the camera at my side as I saw them holding machine guns. I was scared they would confiscate the camera and did not want to be arrested on arrival in Dubai.

When I exited the airport building, the cardiologist, Dr. Yehia, who had been treating Mahmoud for a heart attack that occurred two years earlier, was waiting for me. He greeted me and helped with my luggage. He drove me to his villa, which was subsidized by Rashid Hospital where he worked. I stayed there for a couple of days until Mahmoud's arrival from Doha.

Three weeks later, I relocated to a furnished apartment in the Deira neighborhood. Mahmoud was so generous, he had prepaid the apartment before his departure back to Doha, to allow me to continue my stay in Dubai until my return to Montreal.

The day after I moved to the apartment, I stepped outside the apartment building as the sun was going down. The temperatures were dropping, but it was still extremely hot and humid. Jean, a new friend I made in Ajman, one of the seven Emirates that composed the United Arab Emirates, and the person who issued a sponsorship to allow me to get a visit visa to Dubai, was picking me up for dinner.

As I waited on the sidewalk in front of the building, a white Nissan Patrol stopped in front of me. In it, two young men dressed in traditional Emirati *kandura*, an ankle-length, loose-fitting robe, and *ghutrah*, a local, traditional white headdress, occupied the front seats. The passenger rolled down the window. He was so close; he could have touched me if he wanted to.

"Hello, miss! How are you?" he said in accented English.

I stepped back, remained silent, and looked away. From my time in Syria, I had learned that looking away signalled a desire to not engage in a conversation or get involved.

He continued, "You, beautiful! Please come! Come, we go for drink!"

Although I was ignoring him, he was persistent and continued to try to get me in the car. He then talked to the driver in a local Arabic dialect unfamiliar to me, and they laughed. I was perplexed.

After various attempts, I was getting fearful as there were no pedestrians on the street, and I felt isolated. I looked at him and said, "Mister, if you don't leave now, I will call the police."

They both laughed aloud. He then extended his arm toward me. "Here is my mobile, call the police!" he said, offering me his cellphone.

After having spent almost seven years in Montreal, where threatening to call the police was considered a deterrent, I was not expecting such a reaction at all.

I began to worry. I was not up to the challenge, as I thought these locals must have developed different tools than the Syrians to seduce women.

I slowly stepped backwards while still facing the car until I reached the glass door of the building. I quickly unlocked the door with the key I kept in my hand when I came and went. My mouth was dry, my hands and underarms were sweaty, but I felt a bit safer once I was behind the glass wall.

Seconds later, they gave up and left.

After I reported the incident to Jean, he was not surprised. He told me that the neighbourhood was known for housing prostitutes from Russia. Further, he told me that some apartment buildings in the area were rented with a prostitute as part of the contract. I could not believe my ears. But as I spent more time in Dubai, I came to realize that prostitution was widely popular, practiced behind glamorous glass windows and the dazzling fences of luxurious villas.

Chapter 10

As I continued walking toward my Chicago hotel on the Magnificent Mile, I thought how fortunate I was to be able to walk and feel safe in the streets of one of the largest and most dangerous cities in the United States, without being approached by anyone or groped, as was so often the case on the streets of Damascus. The Syrian men did not miss any opportunity to grab and pinch the thighs of an unveiled girl on a sidewalk.

The first time I was groped, I was 16. I was walking behind Father on the sidewalk of Al-Salhiyie Street. While making my way through the hundreds of men and scarfed women sporting long, beige, and other pale-coloured coats, I felt a painful pinch on my thigh. "Ouch!" I screamed.

Confused, I looked around. It was impossible to identify the perpetrator. I pushed through the crowds to catch up with Father. When I got near him, I said, "Someone just pinched me!"

"Keep walking," he said. "And stay next to me."

Little did I know then that the pinch was the start of a long-lasting struggle with street groping. I could imagine Father knew about the phenomenon but could not openly discuss it with me nor make it stop.

As the pinching practice multiplied with the passage of time, and the street groping increased, I had to figure out what to do about it. I could not remain silent and accept that strangers allowed themselves to meddle with my body without my consent or any consequences.

The blue bruises on my thighs always unlocked a strange desire to fight the unacceptable phenomenon. I was ready to go to war to preserve my dignity!

After I made the decision to fight street offenses, the next time someone groped me, at the same spot where it happened the first time in Damascus, I used my anger to strike back. I turned around, ran after the man, and punched him hard on the shoulder. Surprised, he turned around and shouted with fury, "Sharmouta!"

He did not hit back. It was a moment of victory, even though he was insulting me by calling me a "slut."

Pleased with the results of my improvisation, I adopted the technique as a retaliatory measure. I knew I was taking a risk every time I struck back by hitting the offending man on the back or shoulder. But since I was doing it in the open, I thought I would be safe.

One day, though, it angered one man, who confronted me and hit me back in the face as he yelled, "Sharmouta!" The crowd got involved and stopped him. I was sore for a couple of days, but I was not going to stop because of a bruise on my face and my pride.

My personal war had become even more meaningful. That incident made me more careful but never less determined to continue the battle against inappropriate conduct on the streets. I knew that all girls and women were exposed to the same intolerable behaviour, and I wanted to be a forerunner in addressing it.

The pleasure a man could get by groping a girl on the thigh or the buttocks eluded my understanding. My rage against Syrian male society mounted. I was disgusted and criticized the misbehaviour everywhere I could. However, people were convinced there was nothing to be done to stop it. It was considered a social epidemic.

I might not have stopped it, yet I was sure I had created a scratch on the intertwined fabric of the local society and hoped its dents would expand. I knew I had put myself into situations that could have backfired, but the end justified the means.

In early 1977, when I relocated on a temporary basis to Al-Nabek to start working at the shoe factory, I had mastered my technique. I was no longer scared of the reaction of the men who groped me, and I hit back with a firm fist. I was determined to win the fight.

Located 80 kilometres north of Damascus, Al-Nabek was a small town with less than 20,000 inhabitants. The area was arid, with temperatures over 30 degrees Celsius during daytime, and it had a sandy, desert-like soil with sporadic dusty trees. I had rented a cozy room with old furniture in a long-time family house near the town's square. The room was separated from the family house and was accessed through a short staircase from the courtyard shaded by a fragrant orange tree and with a water fountain in its centre, typical of traditional Syrian architecture in Damascus and its surrounding areas.

Late in the afternoons, to enjoy the cooler breeze of the evenings when the heat dissipated, the town's elderly men would sit and lounge, forming a line on the sidewalk outside the shops surrounding the main square.

One early evening, I went for grocery shopping. To reach the store, I had to cross the square. The elderly men were already lounging comfortably on their chairs enjoying the breeze. I heard the fast steps of someone approaching behind me.

The sound of the steps became louder as the pedestrian passed me. He groped my right thigh and continued walking at the same fast pace as if he had not done anything. I was so disturbed and upset by this behaviour, especially as it happened in front of the reposed elderly, I ran after him and punched him on the back with all the strength I had. He kept walking and did not even look back.

Amazed, I heard the older gentlemen clapping and cheering me. I felt so accomplished at that moment as I smiled and brushed off the humiliation. The news travelled fast in Al-Nabek, and I became famous for hitting a man in the main square. This became a deterrent. Men in Al-Nabek did not grope me anymore. At last, I had mastered the art of dealing with gropers!

Montaha Hidefi

Chapter 11

To get a job at the shoe factory in Al-Sweida, one of four newly planned, government-owned shoe factories in Syria, I had to pass a cognitive test that assessed my abilities in perception, memory, thinking, reasoning, and problem-solving to determine my potential to solve work-related problems. The test was conducted by French experts from the Association pour la Formation Professionnelle de l'Industrie de Chaussures (AFPIC), the Association of Professional Training in the Shoe Industry. It was the most reputed centre for professional training then when France was the leader of the shoe industry.

There were hundreds of applicants from around Syria, but only 28 of us were selected to go to France on a government-subsidized trip to be trained at the AFPIC centres.

Although none of the four factories were built when we left for France in February of 1976, the government had promised employment at one of the factories after the training concluded. In return for the sponsored training in France, we signed contracts that stipulated we would work at any of these factories for five consecutive years. We were so young, none of us cared about the contract stipulations. The most important thing was to travel to France, without our families.

The four months I spent at this early stage of my youth between Cholet, in the west, and Romans, in the southeastern part of France, moulded me.

Based on the results of the cognitive test, I was selected by the French experts from the AFPIC to train in Romans to become a shoe designer. However, Syrian government officials decided to segregate the females from the males during the training period, for fear of mingling and indecent behaviour. Rather than using my potential based on the results of the cognitive test, the government decision was to train me alongside the other females, so they changed my assignment and sent me to Cholet. I came to know of this change when I started my first training day and was told I was to learn how to sew shoes.

That was one of the early, shocking lessons I learned about the Syrian male mentality. Females were not equal to males. They were not evaluated based on their capabilities but based on their gender, and their fate was decided by males, who might be of an inferior intellectual level.

Two months into the training, as I started to master the stitching techniques, I got an unexpected notice from the Syrian officials to relocate to Romans. One of the trainees in Romans was having mental health issues and was incapable of completing his training. They wanted to replace him with someone who had advanced cognitive skills, so they chose me.

My relocation to Romans was a victory. There I was, the only female from the Syrian group to train side by side with the males. It is there where, in less than three months, I learned to speak French and to solve problems based on the method "QOQQC": *Que fait-on? Où le fait-on? Qui le fait-on? Quand le fait-on? Comment le fait-on*? known in English as "the Five W's and How": What is happening? Who is involved? Where does it happen? When does it happen? Why does it happen? How does it happen?

This method had a great influence on my professional and personal life as I applied it in everything I did and continue to do so to this day. It allowed me to solve problems, no matter their size, by dividing them into smaller issues, through the technique of asking questions.

I returned to Syria as a transformed person, competent, skilled, and qualified to face the world with a new European style perspective and a new language skill. The months I spent without my family's supervision taught me to be strong, to depend on my own thought process to face the outside world, and to be me, an unleashed, erupting volcano, motivated to change everything that did not seem right. I felt indestructible at the age of 16.

The years that followed proved that I was not wrong about myself, but I was an innocent teenager, inexperienced in matters of society and cultures. I had to go through life as it unfolded and accept the fact it was mental suicide for a female to challenge an entire society. The road I took, armed with nothing but determination and love for a better life, led me to endless disappointments, heartbreaks, exploitations, mistreatments, and emotional bruises, but I came out of it with a lifetime of knowledge.

When I was in France, I did not experience groping or abuse. Perhaps I was too young. Perhaps I was too naive. Perhaps I was just where I needed to be.

My employment at the shoe factory in Al-Sweida was satisfying for the first years after they relocated me from Al-Nabek. At the age of 17, I was managing the planning department and had three employees reporting to me. They were all older. Over time I developed a friendship with the youngest one of them, Seeham.

Of course, I could not have predicted then the inappropriate conduct of her husband years later, in 1989, when I was working at the Canadian embassy in Damascus.

After graduation in 1988, I obtained my master's in translation and interpretation, an unwavering dream I was determined to achieve since my return from France 12 years earlier. It was the utmost achievement I sought to include in my imaginary toolbox, which was becoming more real every time I added a tangible document to it. One of my professors, Ms. Hanan Al-Malki, wrote me a letter of recommendation and asked me to contact the Canadian embassy, as they were looking for a translator-cum-cultural-assistant and had asked her for recommendations of fresh graduates. She told me she was confident I would be able to get the job. She was right. They hired me. Ms. Al-Malki was another significant influence in my voyage through life. I hope to see her in person one day to acknowledge the enormous impact of her written recommendation on my life after graduation.

I rented an apartment in Mount Mazzeh, the same district where the University of Damascus was located but in a different subdivision. I chose to live in that area due to its proximity to the embassy, which operated at first from the Sheraton Hotel at Umayyad Square, across from Dar Al-Assad for Culture and Arts and later relocated along Al Mazzeh Highway, 10 minutes from the Sheraton.

Mazzeh was one of the most modern and affluent districts of Damascus. I could afford the apartment due to my well-paid position as official translator and cultural assistant at the embassy. I enjoyed my job and knew how fortunate I was to work for such a reputable diplomatic mission. As an interpreter, I accompanied the ambassador to meetings with high government officials, while as an assistant to the cultural attaché, I learned about Canada and participated in the promotion of Canadian culture through participation in "Canada Film Week" and other events related to the arts and culture of the country.

I grew a rich network of locally based diplomatic personnel as well as local journalists, artists, performers, and people that worked in the various cultural centres located in Damascus. After so many years of despair in Syria, the coin was flipped, as I was gaining the respect of the local society. But I always wondered if that was because of me or because of the position I held, since people liked to befriend embassy employees in the hopes of getting *wasta*, kickback, to get foreign visas and leave the country.

Seeham and her husband, Issam, lived in Dwel'a, three kilometres southeast of Damascus. Dwel'a was a bustling town in the greater Damascus metropolitan area with a mostly Christian population.

I used to spend afternoons at Seeham's while Issam was in the United States figuring out how to make a living. When things did not turn out that well for him, he returned to Syria, and soon after, they had a baby boy.

Although Issam came from a well-off, middle-class household, his family did not want him to rely on their wealth and had insisted that he find a job. He was not an educated person, so he bought a VW Golf and licensed it as a taxi.

Giving Voice to My Silence

Issam was over six feet tall and skinny, with a dramatic hawk nose that gave him a Pinocchio allure. Though I did not know him well, he often joined our conversations and expressed his dissatisfaction with the economic and political situation in Syria.

On a dusty, overcast, summer day, I was getting ready to leave their home just as he was about to start his afternoon taxi shift. Seeham suggested he could give me a lift. I agreed, not only because it was difficult to catch a taxi in Dwel'a, but also the transit commute from Dwel'a to Damascus was exceptionally unpleasant, almost hostile, with eventual opportunities for thigh-groping and pinching.

As Issam started driving, I started a friendly conversation. I asked about his plans. He began talking about the difficulties he was having with Seeham. I was respectful and told him that he was a nice person and that he could manage having a good life with Seeham or any other person.

As soon as I finished my sentence, his right hand left the gear stick and landed on my left thigh. I twitched as I shoved his hand away. He started to say how beautiful I was and how he had admired me since the day he met me. I was silent, trying to digest the outrageous statements and innuendo.

"I know a friend who has an apartment not too far from here. We could go and spend the afternoon together," he proposed.

I spoke up. "This is wrong! Seeham is my friend. I have no interest in being your lover."

Surprised by my reaction, he insisted, "But you just said that I was a nice person. Besides, I am having rough time with Seeham, and we could spend time together to make me feel better."

Confused and disappointed, I continued to reject his advances. As soon as we reached the city of Damascus, I asked him to pull over and leave me there. I did not want him to know where I lived. He stopped, and I got out of the vehicle in distress.

As I walked away, I wanted to disappear in the folds of the harsh Syrian reality. I thought how the incident cemented the bitter truth I formulated about Syrian men and which I tried profoundly to refuse to accept with the aim of living in peace in society. I realized the truth about the binary nature of the personality of Syrian men. Their behaviour toward women was a symptom of a psychological disorder deeply rooted in society. In a way, they sought to behave like Western men, to be open-minded, liberated, and sincere. However, the Bedouin traditions embedded in their DNA through hundreds of years of chauvinism and excessive loyalty to the masculine culture was stronger and remained present behind the disguise they presented to the outside world. A substantial number of the Syrian men I met felt entitled to the appropriation of women to whom they were attracted. They were opportunistic. It did not matter if they were married or in a relationship, or if the woman was married or in a relationship, when they felt attracted, they ambushed and attacked their prey.

I never returned to see Seeham. I was unsure how to manage seeing Issam again. I had mixed feelings about being honest with Seeham. I always wondered if she would have believed me had I told her or if they would have separated because of me. The situation was too delicate and complicated. I decided that avoiding any confrontation and breaking the friendship without explanation was best for Seeham and for me. It was a fight-or-flight situation in which I behaved as a coward and deserted the scene without a trace, but I preferred that she keep a nice memory of me and preserve her marriage.

Chapter 12

As the years passed, working at the shoe factory in Al-Sweida was becoming ever more tedious. I was insulting my intelligence by staying in a mundane job amid government politics and red tape while my income was only 350 Syrian pounds a month, less than US$100, which was too low even by the standards of the time.

A mounting desire to rip myself from the corrupted, rotten society of Syria, imposed on me by my parents, inspired me to conceive a plan that proved to be my liberation from the social imprisonment and oppression I felt there. I recognized that to escape the psychological detention imposed by local customs and traditions and the overt sexual innuendos, I needed tools to allow me to leave the country. I created an imaginary toolbox that became a briefcase to accompany me on my journey while in Syria, and beyond. I needed education, post-graduate degrees, and foreign languages. I needed to focus on myself and disregard whatever I was subjected to until the time would be opportune to leave.

With that in mind, and because I interrupted my schooling at the seventh grade to go to France, I home-schooled myself for the pre-secondary education level. Students who did not attend school could study at home and take an exam.

After obtaining the diploma, I had to wait three years before I could pass the exam for the upper secondary education level, known as *baccalaureate*, a prerequisite for admission to university.

Each level of education I attained would be an achievement, a trophy I would toss into my imaginary toolbox to fuel the future I envisioned somewhere outside of Syria. It was my survival kit to accomplish my dream.

I understood my employment at the shoe factory would never lead me to a significant position, though I was holding one of the most important positions as the production planner. But because I was so young, I had many adversaries who wanted to replace me. I set a goal to study French literature at university and become a translator. At this point, I was fluent in Spanish, Arabic, and French and had a functional knowledge of English. A specialization in translation seemed only right, although my passion was for the arts.

The concept of a shoe factory in Al-Sweida, employing a high number of females to stitch and perform other manual functions, was new in the region and had raised rumours about females offering sexual services. Though they were only rumours, people believed them, and look down upon the female workers. People considered the factory a brothel. Young and old, educated, and uneducated men applied to work there to take advantage of the abundance of females.

Like the other women, I also received advances and invitations to go out to "have fun," as they used to say. However, romances did not interest me, and I always refused the invitations.

The contract with the AFPIC expired in 1978. The Syrian government signed a new contract with the Italian company Garditalia, which supplied Italian experts to support the design and production of shoes. The experts were to be based in Al-Sweida, the biggest of the four factories.

The factory general manager organized an employee meeting to take place in the cafeteria on the Italians' first working day to introduce them and explain their approach. Following the introductions, the head of the Italian experts stood up to address the employees and started a speech in Italian that might as well have been a presentation at a convention for the deaf. No one at the factory spoke Italian. We became agitated and wondered how we would collaborate with so-called experts if they could not communicate with us.

Since I spoke Spanish, I could understand parts of the speech. The general manager spotted me nodding and asked me to interpret the speech in Arabic.

Shaking, I said, "I don't speak Italian. Spanish is different."

"You can manage," he said. "We need some help here."

I approached the podium, looked at the Italian expert, and then watched the audience. There were more than 100 employees. All eyes were on me. Moments of silence followed. I could feel the sweat accumulating on my upper lip, and my legs were weak. I simulated a smile.

I took deep breaths, stared at an imaginary void in front of me, and started interpreting in Arabic my understanding of what the Italian expert was saying. Employees started cheering even though I was unsure I was saying the right things.

There was no guarantee I had done an excellent job with the interpretation. Nonetheless, I had just survived my first-ever public speech! It was a smashing success I proudly stored in my imaginary toolbox. Over the years, the toolbox became a survival mechanism that kept me grounded as I looked forward to achieving my dream of leaving Syria.

With the agreement of the general manager, the Italians taught me the Italian language. I took an hour-long lesson every day. The resemblance of Italian to Spanish was such that it was easy to learn, and a month after my first public appearance, I was fluent in Italian. I added another trophy to my toolbox.

Despite the number of achievements collected in my toolbox as time progressed, society did not respect me as an accomplished young woman until I started working at the embassy. The harassment continued. I was just another woman in a male-dominated society. My social status did not improve, and my eagerness to leave the country increased.

Montaha Hidefi

Chapter 13

I was a shrewd, adaptive person, and Garditalia's managers were so pleased with my performance, whether in translations, administration, or production planning, I received an invitation to visit their headquarters in Salò, Italy, less than two hours east of Milan.

I recollect how the Italian men shouted, *"Che bella! Che bella donna!"* How beautiful! What a beautiful woman! as I strolled the lakeside promenade of Lake Garda. In contrast with Syrians, there was no groping or pinching, only shouts of admiration. The soft innuendos that were meant to compliment me could have led to other situations had I taken them in a different context. I felt desired yet safe in Italy.

Over the following years, I visited Salò and the neighbouring city, Gardone Riviera, various times, always at the special invitation of Garditalia's management, and became comfortable speaking in public. I stay connected to this day with the Italian experts and their children.

The success stories I was gathering in my imaginary toolbox sparked further motivation to obtain my baccalaureate and start university. I studied for three years at a comfortable pace while maintaining my job at the shoe factory.

Yasmine, a married friend of mine in Al-Kafr, was also preparing for the baccalaureate exam. Her husband was an Arabic language teacher. They had a two-year-old, adorable girl and a baby boy. After work, I often went to their home, and we studied together. Her husband helped us with Arabic grammar and syntax.

One fine day, we were so involved with conjugation tables, I did not pay attention to the time. Night had fallen when I set out for home. In the absence of streetlights and without a flashlight to illuminate the way, visibility was minimal. I accelerated my pace, as I was feeling afraid of the darkness and fearful that someone could emerge from the shadows.

I heard footsteps approaching in the distance. My heart was pounding at a thousand beats per second. My mouth dried. I was trembling at the thought of an unknown stalker in the darkness.

Seconds later, a shadow started to materialize, and a young man appeared through the folds of darkness. He stopped right in front of me! It was Faysal. He lived on the other side of the village. In small villages such as Al-Kafr, everybody knew everybody.

He greeted me with a melodic, *"Massa alkhair!"* with an elongated "aaaaa," which meant he was pleased to see me. "Good evening! What are you doing here?" he asked.

"I was studying at Yasmine's," I replied, concealing my anxiety.

"How was the studying?" he asked and continued with other insignificant questions.

My brain was working out an escape plan as I sensed an inevitable assault, so his words sounded like indistinct utterances. I could not figure out how to get rid of him. He stepped forward and got so close his face almost touched mine. I stepped back, almost losing my balance. He then leaned forward in a gesture to kiss me, by force.

I would not consent to such a kiss! He was forcing himself on me. I could feel the temperature of his oily face near mine. I tried to push him away, but he was much stronger than me.

I struggled. I was unprepared, carrying a pile of books in my left arm. I pushed him with all my strength, but he would not move. I wanted to smack him, but I had lost my advantage. So instead of a slap, I scratched his face with my long nails. He lost balance, yelped, and held his hand to his face.

I cannot remember when or how I started running. I did not stop until I got home, close to 10 minutes later. I was quivering and breathless as if I had gone through a snowstorm. And I was angry.

Next day, Zakadi, a teenager who lived near Faysal's house and was a good friend of ours, came to visit. As I recounted the story, she mentioned she had seen him in the morning, and he had a visible scar on his cheek. I felt satisfied to have afflicted him with a physical laceration. He deserved it. I hoped he learned a lesson.

I never saw him or spoke to him ever again. I had a profound sense of pride for striking back every time someone attempted to physically harass me and take advantage of me.

Montaha Hidefi

Chapter 14

Friday, July 13, 2018. What a sad day it was.

Kevin, a friend of Michael's, in his early forties, had passed away from a heart attack the previous Saturday. Michael asked me to accompany him to the Gilbert MacIntyre Funeral Home in Guelph, Ontario, to attend a commemoration of his life.

As we stepped inside, I realized the only thing I knew about funeral homes came from the television show *Six Feet Under*. I had never been inside a funeral home. Although I had previously seen deceased people, it was not in that type of setting.

There was a crowd of around 300 people in the hall. I knew Kevin through Michael and had seen him only once, seven years earlier. Listening to his close family members and friends speaking at the podium about their memories of him depressed me. I wept.

I was experiencing a sensation of worthlessness. We are born, we grow, we study, we work, we love, we struggle, we suffer, we have kids, we make money, we travel, we author books, we paint, we dream, we want to live, we want to be. And suddenly, we die! All that remains of us is dust, and the memories we create with others.

Sadness was stirring the deepest hollows of my heart. I remained almost crippled that entire afternoon and was unable to function.

I remembered the tragic death of my uncle Fuad, Mother's brother, in a car accident on the road to Damascus. It happened a few years after we arrived in Al-Kafr. They transported his body from the hospital in an ambulance in a lightweight, wooden crate. On arrival at the town's wake room, they pulled his body out of the vehicle and put him to rest on a mattress lying on the floor in the centre of the room. The body was stiff. A chequered, red-and-white Arabic headdress called *hatta* covered his face and head to avoid showing his shattered face. This hatta colour was his favourite. During the wake, I was sitting on the floor next to Mother, near his covered head. I could see the blood soaking through the hatta on the left side of what was his face. Although I was too young to know my uncle well, as I set next to his chequered, ball-headed, inert body, listening to the sobs of the women in that mortuary ritual made me cry. I passed out multiple times from acute abdomen pain. The upheaval and stress of that event lasted throughout my youth. The distorted image of my uncle's face remained imprinted on my mind, and I could see it every time I closed my eyes. It had traumatized me so much that since then I have avoided seeing the dead.

Suddenly, it occurred to me that on this same day, in 2010, we relocated to Guelph. I had landed a new job as the marketing manager for North America at an Austrian powder coatings company and had to start the following day. I had lost my previous job in The Netherlands as global strategic colour consultant at a reputable German special effect pigments manufacturer earlier that year, owing to the economic meltdown.

Coming back to Canada after 11 years of being an expat was thrilling. I was fond of my new employer and was enthusiastic about reconnecting with marketing in a field I was familiar with, powder coatings.

My long-lasting romance with the coatings industry began in Dubai. In those early days, the only condition for a foreigner to remain in Dubai was to have a job, which granted the issuance of a residence visa. Although Dubai was a typical Middle Eastern city, surrounded by sand and bursting with palm trees and camels crossing the highways freely, there was something unique and difficult to fathom about it. It had a strange appeal to me even though, when I left Syria, I made a promise to myself to never again live in an Arab country.

Dubai was a charming piece of desert bustling with Indians and workers from the subcontinent and was still little known in the 1990s. Westerners did not even know where it was on a map or how to pronounce its name. With its 39 storeys, the 149-metre-tall Dubai World Trade Centre white tower was then the tallest building in the Arab world. Inaugurated by Queen

Elizabeth in 1979, it still stands tall in the Dubai sky next to the new trade centre, a building of historical significance commemorating the fast growth of one of the most modern cities in the world today.

Once I decided to look for a job in Dubai, it took just a week before Nadia Recruitment Agency got me an interview with Ali Al-Bawardy, chair of Al-Bawardy Investments, which had interests in Spinneys Supermarkets. They were looking for an administrative assistant. Although I had just completed my graduate studies in business administration at the University of Sherbrooke, my plan was to get any job that provided a residence visa and later search for the right opportunity at my own pace.

Days later, I got an offer for the job with an income of 6,500 Emirati dirhams per month, the equivalent of CAN$2,300. A bit less than what I was earning in Montreal; however, considering there was no income tax, I was banking the entire income.

The job functions were primitive, and when Ali was out of the office, which was frequently, there was nothing to do except count the hours. I took that opportunity to organize his filing system and get rid of old letters that had sat in folders for years, while keeping an eye on job announcements in the newspapers.

After five months of employment with Al-Bawardy, Nadia Recruitment arranged for an interview in Jebel-Ali Free Zone with a reputed American company in the chemicals industry. Gerard, the French-national sales manager interviewed me. I thought the interview went well; we spoke in English and French. A week later I received an invitation for a second interview with Angelo, the managing director.

An Italian-national, Angelo was very professional. We spoke in English and Italian during the interview. The following week, Nadia's office called, notifying me of a job offer for the position of office manager with a monthly income of 7,500 dirhams, US$300 more than my income at Al-Bawardy.

The additional income was not the main driver to accept the offer. Rather, the key motivation was the prospects that were suddenly available to me by working for such a company, providing my first, but not last, experience with a multinational.

I learned from Angelo about the business through discussions and meetings while from Gerard, I learned prospecting and selling. Two well-informed coaches, to whom I owe my primary knowledge in the chemicals and coatings industry, surrounded me.

I was progressing at light speed. Since I did not have much to do in my private life in Dubai and did not know many people, I would go to the office on weekends. Angelo noticed my contributions to the organization. Consequently, my income started growing steadily. Two years later, I had almost doubled my salary.

Besides my responsibilities as office manager, I did customer service support and dealt with key accounts on the phone. Angelo and Gerard invited me regularly to accompany them to customer visits in Dubai, so I could learn more about them. I showed a high interest in the sales area and wanted to advance in that direction. At the same time, I was interested in knowing more about how to run a business across borders since the office was responsible for the market throughout the Middle East.

Things were going very well for me in Dubai. I was happy and my job was fulfilling. In addition, I met a sea captain from Denmark, and we got married on Valentine's Day in 1998, less than two months after we met at a party. Even though marriage was not a priority in my life due to my relationship failures, I thought if I were to marry it was a suitable time, especially since I had fallen in love with Lars, and he proposed.

Since Lars was mostly absent from home as he navigated the waters of oceans and seas around the world, I spent most my time wrapped in my work and took on additional responsibilities in sales. I started visiting customers in all countries of the Middle East and attended business meetings in France, Italy, and other European countries.

Giving Voice to My Silence

One day, our biggest customer in the region, a Norwegian paints company, had organized an all-day strategic meeting that included attendees from their offices in Dubai and Norway and the company's counterparts from Dubai, France, and Germany. Angelo insisted I attend the meeting, which would provide me with additional exposure as I was becoming more immersed in sales.

The meeting did not go as well as anticipated. The company officials demanded services that were beyond our ability to fulfill. As we broke for lunch, our main contact, Geir, purchasing manager for the Middle East, sat across the table. Angelo was to my left and Gerard was to my right.

It was the first time I met with Geir, though not the last. He was a golfer and used metaphors related to golf to explain his viewpoint. Although he appeared soft and quiet, he was hyperactive and loud.

Angelo loved to boast about me and my achievements to customers. He told Geir that I had an MBA from Canada.

Sporting a malevolent smile as he looked at me, Geir replied with a question. "Do you know what MBA means?" He cracked a loud laugh and said, "Married but available!"

My immediate desire was to reach out and smack him! Angelo gave me a kick under the table to keep me quiet.

Although we had a company policy that condemned harassment, even from customers, Angelo wanted me to be submissive. We were in a strategic meeting with our most important customer, and I would have ruined the outcome had I reacted negatively. But I did not share my superior's viewpoint.

Nobody at the table commented on this insulting, verbal harassment. I remained calm and continued my lunch, but deep inside I was boiling.

When we returned to the office the following day, Angelo told me about the expectations of accepting comments from customers. He inducted me into the corporate world, which included harassment and misbehaviour.

The following year, as I started dealing directly with Geir as my key customer, I got to hear his golf-inspired metaphors.

Geir's desk was always clear of any item. His approach to doing business in 1999 preceded the concept of paperless. He rudely told suppliers, including me, "If you want to send me something, send it by email. Otherwise, I won't read it." This might sound normal today; however, in those days most business communication happened through fax.

There were so many complaints about Geir's negative attitude, superiority complex, and disrespect to suppliers, he was relocated back to Norway and soon after was dismissed, from what I heard.

Arvid, Geir's successor, was the complete opposite. He was nice and cared about suppliers. We built a good, professional relationship and remain friends to this day.

In 2001, the manager responsible for the Middle East, who was based in Sophia Antipolis on the French Riviera, had approved a budget for me to pursue a post-graduate program at the Australian University of Wollongong in Dubai, where I would acquire a master's degree in international business. Another achievement to add to my imaginary toolbox that had by then transformed into a briefcase filled with awards and trophies I carried with me around the world.

At the beginning of 2003, the company decided to shut down the operations in the Middle East, and my position was abolished. They proposed to relocate me to France, which I declined, as the position was not on par with my career plans, and they did not offer an attractive compensation package.

I was going through stressful times. Lars and I decided to divorce since, in the previous five years of marriage, we spent little time together owing to his and my travelling schedules. We were mostly on the road. I was about to lose my job, and I participated in many graduation projects that required a lot of my attention. I decided to remain in Dubai and looked for another job.

Giving Voice to My Silence

Two months later, I had two offers of employment in hand, one from a previous customer and one from one of my professors at university. Then, Arvid called to notify me about a new opening in marketing at their sister company in powder coating. Up until then, I was unfamiliar with powder coatings, and although I had just completed my master's majoring in marketing, I had never had a full-time job in marketing. I applied, nevertheless.

Soon after, I received an invitation for an interview with Larry, regional vice-president for the Middle East. The interview was positive, and Larry offered me the opportunity to venture into two areas I was unfamiliar with: powder coatings and marketing. I accepted the challenge and took the job, to start later in August.

Larry's brother, Bruce, was the regional vice-president for Southeast Asia at the same company. Bruce had a distinctive character than Larry. His personality, behaviour, and actions implied an inferiority complex and exuded mistrust. He constantly tried to prove himself in business; however, I did not always appreciate his decisions.

Despite his traits and my doubts about his way of running the business, I had a courteous professional relationship with him, or so I thought.

In my position as global marketing manager, I was required to travel to all company locations in 11 countries around the world, including Thailand, where Bruce was based.

Bruce's nephew, Garry, worked in Thailand in sales with responsibilities for Southeast Asia. We developed a respectful, professional relationship. In one of my business trips to Thailand, he disclosed a very disturbing matter to me. Bruce was referring to me in meetings and other company events as "Miss Boobs." This disturbed Garry but he explained it was not his place to discuss it with his uncle.

I did not mention anything to Bruce, but when I returned to Dubai, I decided not to remain silent about the misconduct. I reported the matter to Larry and requested that Bruce cease that type of disrespectful behaviour at once. Else, I was going to escalate the matter to headquarters in Norway.

The next time Bruce was in Dubai, he knocked at the glass door of my office. With a hand gesture I invited him in. He entered and closed the door behind him. He sat in front of me, looked me in the eyes, and said, "I am sorry. I was wrong. I will not say this again."

For the following two years, I limited my contact with Bruce to only important business matters. I no longer wanted to communicate with him. I had unpleasant feelings for him and did not trust him.

Remarkably, the powder coatings company I started to work at in Guelph was presided over by Larry, who relocated to Canada in 2006. The coatings industry is like a bubble filled with liquid. Inside it, everybody swims in the same waters. Everybody knows everybody. People transfer from one company to another and meet again.

One afternoon of 2016, I was sitting in my office in Guelph. Larry entered and said, "Guess who is here?"

I could not believe my eyes when I saw Bruce coming in. It had been many years since I last saw him or spoke to him. I hesitated but stood up and shook hands with him and was uncomfortable for the short length of time he stood there. My stomach was churning, I felt nauseous and almost vomited, just recalling what he had called me in the past.

Wrongful conduct in the workplace is disguised under countless covers. I recall back in 2010, a month or two after I started the job in Guelph, I attended a sales management meeting. My boss, Dan, vice-president for sales and marketing, chaired the session. In his opening of the meeting, referencing Maslow's basic human survival needs, he said, "What a man can be, he must be!" Then he went on to elucidate that when a man meets a woman, the first thing that crosses his mind is something like, "Is she interested in me? And, if not, how do I get her to have sex with me?"

Giving Voice to My Silence

I was stunned to have heard this introductory statement, especially since I was the only woman in the room. Most colleagues looked at me with tight-lipped smiles. I felt uncomfortable and was unsure if it was appropriate to say something, as I did not know the culture of the company that well. I looked down at the floor and remained silent. No one commented, and the meeting continued.

The years passed by, and I noticed that my boss often used metaphors with sexual connotations during meetings. He tagged his allegories to business gurus very few of us seemed to recognize. Although I always supported the notion of not accepting such inappropriate insinuations, I felt uncomfortable to speak up to my boss for fear of being dismissed, even though I had a good, professional relationship with him and was honest and open in addressing him when it came to business matters.

The last time I heard him using sexual allusions as a metaphor, it was during a townhall meeting in the Guelph office, where around 50 employees from the night shift in production were gathered in a circle.

When it was Dan's turn to lead the conversation, he started the session by asking, "How many of you have had a fight with your other half?" Multiple hands were raised. Following with other questions, he concluded with, "How many of you had the best sex of your life the night after having a big fight with your other half?" While most employees giggled and started making "Yeah!" sounds, most of us looked at our footwear to hide our embarrassment. He had performed the same routine the previous month at the Illinois site with more than 100 employees present.

After the meeting was over, I called for a debrief as part of the organizing team. Dan could not join us for the debrief as he had to address another important matter. It was at the debrief that the human resource director and the CFO, who passed away in early 2021 after a short but serious fight against cancer, pointed out that such rhetoric was considered sexist and unacceptable at the workplace and that it had to stop. Next morning when I briefed Dan, he was unhappy to get this feedback and told me privately that he felt his language was ordinary and that the HR director and the CFO were opposing him because they did not like him.

I was filled with satisfaction that two women at the same corporate level as Dan stood up for all employees of the company, although in his and their absence. It is not unusual to hear about corporate executives that use gender prejudice in the workplace without considering the consequences or even thinking of it as wrongdoing.

In parallel, in October of 2010, Clemens, the company's global CEO in Austria, invited me to attend a global "vision retreat" in China. This was an annual gathering where high-ranking executives from around the world met in a friendly atmosphere to experience team-building and draft future visions for the company. During a relaxed session that included me, Clemens, and his life-long mentor, Hemmedinger, Clemens stated that had he not been observing an abstinence month, he would have envisioned other things happening between us.

Stunned by the blunt statement, I smiled and kept quiet. In such an unexpected situation, it was difficult to take a stand. I had been caught off guard by the highest-ranking executive at the company. We never discussed his comment in the years that followed, nor did he ever make any other inappropriate insinuations after that.

Although these incidents might sound insignificant and meaningless to some, we all must learn how not to remain silent in similar situations. We must learn how to face the offender or talk to someone who can face the offender. Otherwise, it festers and becomes difficult to eradicate.

Chapter 15

The ceremony of my wedding to Lars took place in the Holy Trinity Church of Dubai. A small group of friends were in attendance.

While I grew up not believing in God or religion, I was aware of the family religious values I was breaking by marrying an *ajnabi*, a foreigner. But since I had broken many conventional rules before, religion was not going to stop me from being with the man I chose to be with. Besides, being residents of Dubai, we only had two choices to marry while in the country and have the marriage legally registered in Dubai, either at church or by a Muslim imam. We decided on the church.

The following month, I sent a picture of the wedding to my sister Danela and another friend in Syria, who I trusted would not disclose the news to my family.

I could not announce my marriage to Mother and Father as I feared the consequences of being killed at the hands of someone they would hire, as it was not permitted in the Druze religion for a woman to marry a Christian or a member of any other religious community.

Even after so many years had passed, I had not forgotten the anguish from an incident that happened once in front of our house in Al-Kafr.

It was 1978, and I was then dating Adham from Al-Sweida. He was a year older than me. We were introduced by a common acquaintance the previous year and fell in love. He was an orphan. He lost his mother as a child, and his father had abandoned them. Nobody knew where his father was. His aunt had raised him, his sister, and two half-siblings.

His aunt loved him beyond imagination. Three years earlier, she paid for his trip to Spain to go look for his father, as he heard he was living there. When he came back without finding him, he was incredibly sad. One night he told his aunt he wished to have a vehicle. Next morning when he woke up, he found a briefcase filled with money next to his pillow. His aunt told him to get the vehicle he wanted. He got himself a white Opel Ascona.

As he lived in Al-Sweida and I lived in Al-Kafr, we agreed to meet Sunday and Tuesday evenings. He would pick me up in front of our house after darkness had fallen, and we would secretly go to his house and spend the evening there. He would then drop me back home, and I would sneak into my room quietly so as not to alert my family about my absence. This arrangement worked well, and only Danela knew about my night escapades. Even though he was Druze, we had to keep our relationship in the dark. The Druze society forbid public romances.

One day, Adham decided to go to Venezuela to look for his father, as someone had informed him, he was there. I was extremely sad to see him go but could not change his mind. I was so much in love with him, I promised him I would be waiting for him at our secret meeting spot.

The months passed and I tirelessly waited for him every Sunday and Tuesday evening at the gate of our house. He never showed up, nor did he send a letter. I ended up weary of waiting to no avail, so I decided to stop my routine of waiting at the gate.

Months later, he called to say I was not out waiting for him when he had come the previous Tuesday, as I had promised. I explained the situation, and we agreed to meet again the following Sunday.

He had found his father, and they travelled together from Venezuela. Adham and I started seeing each other again. As he had sold his car before leaving for Venezuela, his father bought a burgundy Mercedes-Benz 280c.

One evening, when he stopped the vehicle by our entrance gate, I leaned at his window before hopping in, and we exchanged greetings. I noticed an elderly man walk by, wearing a traditional black *sherwal*, Aladdin pants, and a black jacket. I recognized he was from House Hidefi, though not related to my family. He lived down the road in our neighbourhood. As he passed

Giving Voice to My Silence

the vehicle, Adham and I continued our chat and did not pay attention to him.

When I got in the car seconds later, the scent emanating from the new, black leather seats and dashboard caressed my nostrils. I felt immersed in a sensual pleasure as the fragrance draped our tender encounter in a flawless moment of affection. Adham started driving slowly, not far behind the man.

We were still chatting when the man turned toward us. Through the stream of the light beams we noticed he had a gun in his right hand, pointed at us.

Adham braked. I screamed, *"Shou hedha?"* What is this?

The man continued walking toward us with the gun still pointed at us. I shouted, *"Souk, souk!"* Drive, drive!

We were both petrified. The anxiety mounted. My legs were quaking, my heart rate accelerated, and I wanted to hide my face in my hands but also wanted to keep watching what the man would do. Adham kept composed as he looked ahead, thinking how to manage the situation. Death walked in our direction, but we did not know how to stop it, or even defend ourselves.

At my directive, Adham continued driving toward the man, who came closer and closer. Then, the crack of gunfire ripped the evening of its silence. I looked at Adham, and then started checking for wounds as the second burst of gunfire, followed by a third and fourth, ruptured the stillness of that lovely evening.

The man jumped aside to prevent being run over as Adham continued past him. Then, we heard another gunshot and the bullet flew past Adham's ear, streaked his left cheek, and left a hole on the windshield as it exited the car.

Adham covered his cheek with his left hand and kept driving. We were terrified! The man emptied his chamber, firing the last bullet.

Adham hit the accelerator and we disappeared into the gloom of the street ahead. We were speechless.

I was quivering and wanted to know if Adham was wounded. Miraculously, his cheek was not bleeding intensely. He drove silently, leading us outside Al-Kafr. Five minutes later, we reached Hubran, a small village south of Al-Kafr. From there on, to avoid the villagers' attention, he turned his headlights off and took a dirt road until there were no more houses and only the stars lighting our way. He finally stopped.

He looked at me and took my hands in his. Shaking he asked, *"Beeke shee, hayatee?"* Are you okay, my life?

Not knowing if we were hurt, we looked for blood on each other's face and at our clothes. Except for the thin stripe of blood on Adham's face, we did not find any other evidence of blood. We looked at each other and exhaled deeply.

He hugged me and said, *"Al-hamdillah al-salama!"* Thank God you are safe!

We had just escaped a shooting in a residential area of Al-Kafr. Such a thing was unimaginable. The only reason we could think of for the man's behaviour was that it might have looked to him as though we were exchanging affection in public.

Almost paralyzed by anxiety and fear, we were unable to figure out how to deal with the situation. I wanted to go back home, but we were worried that the entire neighbourhood might have been alerted, and we would be faced with reinforcements and more gunfire. We decided to spend the night in the vehicle under the stars. We had no water, food, or covers. It was a tough night, interrupted only by our sad sighs. We spoke little and pondered much.

As the night was cracked by the first rays of dawn, Adham drove back toward Al-Kafr. We did not want to be fugitives. Unaware of what awaited us, Adham took the street leading to my house. Everything was quiet and the street was empty.

Adham dropped me home and left at once. I walked, with caution, the 30-metre paved driveway that separated the street from the house, so as not to alert my parents. When I reached my room's door at the front porch, I inserted the key and turned it softly. I slowly opened the door so it would not squeak and entered the room on tiptoe. I did not hear any voices coming from inside.

I quickly changed into my sleeping clothes, opened the door leading to the hall, and went to the bathroom to freshen up. Minutes later, when I went to the kitchen to prepare food before I went to work, Father and Mother were already there. Everything seemed normal and they did not mention anything about the previous night. I presumed they were unaware. I was relieved. I brushed off my distressed feelings, changed my clothes, and went to work.

I was still troubled and scared. I expected at any moment someone would show up to kill me. In the days and weeks that followed, I anticipated that someone would mention something about the incident, but nobody did. Nobody has ever said anything about that night. Adham and I folded the wrinkled memory of it and threw it in the chasm of the past.

Ever since, I have thought of that ill-fated night and tried to analyze it to understand the man's motive. I do believe that the narrow-minded man could not tolerate seeing two young people of opposite genders having a conversation. Although we were not even touching each other when he saw us, as I was outside the vehicle and Adham was behind the wheel, he must have perceived us doing something wrong. His nomadic mentality, measured by different social standards, must have made him feel that he had to preserve the honour of the clan, as it was customary to do.

But why was he carrying a gun? Al-Kafr was a quiet village with no history of violence. Had he seen us in a previous encounter and decided to terminate us?

Had he murdered us that night, he would not have been charged with any wrongdoing; it would have been considered an honour killing, based on the belief that I had brought shame upon the family and violated the principles of the Druze community. It would have been deemed a legal assassination.

Montaha Hidefi

Chapter 16

Sometimes, I wondered if I was a blunder in the ripples of time. Otherwise, why have I had to endure so much abuse and emotional hurt from all layers of society?

My relocation to Canada in September of 1991 was an escape route that I thought would lead me to a society free of exploitation and corruption. It was the primary accomplishment of all achievements I gathered dearly in my imaginary toolbox for so many years.

Alas, gender bias, frequently concealed under sheets of pretention and self-importance, materializes in the most unexpected places.

Two years after I relocated to Montreal, I applied for an opening at the Egyptian consulate as an assistant to the consul general and as a translator. My first interview with the attaché went extremely well, and since I had qualifying experience from my employment at the Canadian embassy in Damascus, I thought I would be offered the job immediately.

The following week, I received an invitation for a second interview with the consul general. I thought the interview also went well, as the consul expressed his satisfaction and praised my experience.

I received a call the following week and they asked me to go back to the consulate for another meeting. When I went, the attaché asked me to write two diplomatic letters in French addressed to the Ministry of Justice in Quebec City. The letters were a plea to cancel parking tickets two diplomats from the consulate had received. I composed the letters in a brief time. When I was done so, they told me they were part of a test to verify my qualifications.

I waited a couple of weeks but did not hear back. I was keen to get the job as it would have allowed me to continue my career in the diplomatic field. I called to check if they selected me. They told me I was, albeit not for the position I had applied for but as a consular secretary, dealing with the public's consular affairs, next to an already existing secretary.

I accepted the consular secretary job thinking that if I got a foot inside, I would be able to reach upper echelons later. The income was much lower. However, I put more emphasis on the status attached to working in the diplomatic field than on the financial compensation.

Once I started the job, I met Magda, the girl they hired for the position for which I had originally applied. She was of Egyptian origin, had just relocated from the United States, was fluent in English, did not speak French, and translation was not her forte. She was tall and thin, with a dark complexion, and wore a Mireille Mathieu bowl-cut hairdo. She presented herself professionally and was well-spoken.

Days later, Magda asked me to prepare for the consul general a daily press summary, in Arabic, based on the local French newspapers. Since she did not speak French, she was unable to perform the task. I knew they were taking advantage of my qualifications without paying for it.

I did the translation and passed it to her. Her office was on the second floor of the building, the same floor as all the diplomats, while I sat at the ground floor in the reception area. Half an hour later, the phone on my desk rang. It was the consul general asking me to get to his office "immediately." I was uncomfortable with his request. He had a frightening demeanour. He was short, dark-skinned, and bold. He tended to look down on people. He came to the office late and left early.

I was worried the translation did not meet his expectations and thought he would reprimand me. I rushed upstairs to his office, knocked on the door, and waited until I heard his voice inviting me to enter. I stepped in and stood in front of his desk.

He looked at me with a big smile and said, "Come! Come with me to the balcony." He took a folder from his desk and opened the balcony door. I followed him.

Giving Voice to My Silence

He sat on one of two white straw chairs divided by a straw tea table. He asked me to sit on the other chair. Although the sun was shining, it was a cold, moist morning. I was not expecting to sit outside, so I did not grab my jacket before I went upstairs. I shivered from the cold and from anxiety. I sat at the edge of the chair and did not look directly at him. I could not figure out what he wanted. I did not have a good feeling about it. I sensed something wrong was about to happen.

He looked at me and said, "Thank you very much for the translation. From today on, I want you to come in person with the translation and read it to me. Can you read this now?"

I was confused. I took the document out of the folder he handed me and started reading the translation I had prepared. He was interrupting me with questions about the topics I was reading about and sometimes asked my opinion.

When I finished, he said, "Thank you. I will see you tomorrow. But do not come until I call you."

I went back to my desk and could not make sense of what had happened. Why did he want me to prepare and read a daily press summary? Was he unable to read, or was that a move to seduce me? What about Magda? Press summaries were part of her job description, not mine.

The daily press summary became a routine. Every morning, when he was ready, he called me to go upstairs, and I would read it to him. During our brief meetings on his balcony, he smoked his cigar and drank Turkish coffee while listening to the news I narrated. After I finished, he would start talking about other things. He would ask me about Montreal or about my family. Sometimes it was a banal conversation, so insignificant I am unable to recall the topics after so many years.

In one instance, he came clean about the reason for not selecting me for the position as his assistant and translator. He said it was because I was a pretty woman and that my beauty would have raised the Egyptian community's eyebrows, and they would start accusing him of having an affair with his assistant.

According to him, having an "ugly" assistant, as he had described Magda, was better for him in front of the community.

I did not understand the logic behind his decision, nor do I now, but I had to accept what he said without discussion as a sign of respect to his position as the head of the consular mission. Whoever I talked to about this, supposed he was power-hungry. Undoubtedly, he had prioritized his status over workplace ethics.

One morning, about three months later, the other consular secretary was absent, and I was dealing with individuals who came to pick up their renewed passports or their legalized commercial documents. My phone rang. It was him, asking me to go upstairs to read the press summary.

"I am sorry, sir," I said, "I can't come right now. There are too many people at the reception, and I am alone."

His scream came at me like a hurricane spilling rage out of the handset. "You do not decide what to do at the consulate! When I tell you to come to see me, you come to see me! I do not care if there are million people at the reception. You must come now!"

I felt so insignificant, I shrank to the size of an ant. Not only was I insulted and disrespected, but he stripped me of my right to defend myself. In my position, my goal was to provide good, timely service to the people that visited the consulate daily; however, the house master's priorities were different.

I left my desk, made my way through the people in the hall, and went upstairs to his office. He was terribly upset and did not hide it. I tried to explain to him the importance of providing good service, but he did not want to listen to me. His main concern was that I had disobeyed him. He clarified that everybody at the consulate was to abide by his orders and that I had disrespected him by challenging his order.

Once I realized he was stuck on his viewpoint, I listened silently to what he had to say. He did not want me to read the press summary, so I went back downstairs feeling I had

Giving Voice to My Silence

been struck by a train. The rest of the day was difficult. I picked up my broken mental fragments but was unable to put them together and function properly.

The next day, I waited all day for his call to come read the press summary. But he did not call. I went home after work feeling beaten up. I spent the entire evening pondering the incident. I reviewed every word I said and its tone. I did not think I disrespected him in any manner. I was unable to comprehend the reason for his violent reaction. After close consideration, I decided I had to contemplate my options.

I did not want a megalomaniac Egyptian diplomat to emotionally enslave me, no matter the salary they were paying me. I knew who I was and what I wanted from a job, and such conduct was not acceptable.

The following morning, I called an hour after the usual start of the workday and asked the secretary to tell the consul general that I quit.

Montaha Hidefi

Chapter 17

There was a time in my life when I never accepted any type of misconduct, even if it was minimal. I am not sure how or when I became complaisant, accepting inappropriate behaviour at the workplace.

In Quebec, it was common for men to address women as *"petite madame"* or "little missus" when they did not want to address them by name.

In 1995, I took a part-time job as a sales assistant in Montreal, at a company specializing in professional cleaning supplies and sanitation equipment. This followed the period of domestic violence I experienced for over three consecutive years, at the end of which I thought I would never be able to stand on my feet again.

I shared the office with another sales assistant, and we occupied a small hall connected to the office of Pierre, the national sales manager. The salespeople often came to the office to discuss their concerns with Pierre or pick up catalogues.

One time, a salesperson came to the office and said, *"Bonjour petite madame!"*

I felt that addressing a woman as "little missus" was demeaning. It was a way of ridiculing her and labelling her as inferior. I was unaccustomed to be addressed in that way, so I felt offended.

I stood up and asked him, "Do you see how tall I am? I am not "petite" at all!"

Everybody in the surrounding area who watched the event unfold was surprised. Shocked, his face turned red, and he apologized, almost crying.

At the time, I was seeing a psychologist to help me deal with my emotional, post-violence, post-traumatic condition to regain self-esteem. I was a broken person, and I was conscious of it. I did not want to continue allowing others to take advantage of me or treat me as diminutive. I wanted to take ownership of who I was as a person and as a female.

The news of the incident travelled throughout the company in no time. Employees considered my reaction as inappropriate, an open attack against the nicest person in the sales force. They did not feel he was offensive, and other women liked the way he addressed them.

Despite others' reactions, I did not feel I was wrong. I would do the same if it happened again. I refused and will always refuse someone to address me as "little missus."

Chapter 18

We would agree the cruellest form of abuse, whether physical, psychological, sexual, or financial, in-person or virtual, is when it is not evident to anyone other than the recipient, and, in cases, the perpetrator. When the recipient hides the shameful fragments of the abusive behaviour in a hidden pod, and does not share the details with others, it confers the wrongdoer increased power to continue the offensive exercise of control over the victim with no fear of retribution.

Covert misconduct - that which is camouflaged by colourful ribbons and manoeuvred behind well-conceived plots and ruses, such as a compliment about one's attire, wrapped in kindness; a discrete touch of the hand; or a seemingly innocent invitation to a cup of coffee - is the most inflammatory, because the recipient, depending on her age and previous experience, is fundamentally unable to recognize the act as a red flag.

Based on my personal experience, I concluded that no female is ever born with the capacity to decode the true meaning behind innuendos she is exposed to the first time in her life. During my childhood and early adolescence, sexual innuendos sounded like music to my ears. They flattered me and made me feel enchanted. I liked the attention from others.

My decoding skills eventually became honed through repeated unsolicited advances from men of all ages. As I grew older, I learned that seduction techniques follow similar patterns shared among the masculine community, as if they had attended the same training seminar or read the same user's manual.

As my life journey took me around the world, by pure serendipity, I realized that no matter where I went, I was the subject of unsolicited stares and advances from men and, on certain occasions, from women. I began to recognize that this form of conduct, or misconduct, transcended geographical and cultural boundaries and spread like a virus festering amid the population of a specific category of people: those seeking to gain self-worth through the assertive control they wielded over their prey.

Before parting with Syria, I painted in my mind a colourful landscape of a world outside Syria where exploitation did not exist. A world that valued women for their intellectual capacities. A world that respected women as human beings. A world that perceived women's voices as words of wisdom. With all the events that manifested in my life leaving scars that will only heal with my death, I came to recognize that my perception was light years off course.

If there was a scale to quantify the most abusive people in my life, I would place Mother as first on the list. I ponder how she disfigured my being from an early age. Her abusive actions continued into my twenties and until I left Syria.

Even after so many years, I have never been able to erase the memory of one afternoon in Al-Kafr in 1977, when her anger created an uproar at home. I was visiting for a couple of days while working in Al-Nabek. She walked slowly into my room and declared, "People are saying you go get drunk in Damascus at night."

"What people?" I asked.

"Samaritans," she said, with a frown.

"And you believe this nonsense?" I questioned.

"Nonsense? You want to deny your night trips with men to Damascus to get drunk?" she insisted as her voice became louder.

"Who, in their right mind, would believe that a person would need to go from Al-Nabek to Damascus, and back, to get drunk at night?" I clarified. "If I wanted to get drunk at night, I would do it in Al-Nabek. Why would I bother to go to Damascus?"

"No! I do not believe you! Everybody is saying you are a "slut"!" she confirmed, furious. She started pacing back and forth, in and out of the room.

"I am a slut?" I yelled. "You believe your Samaritans against my word? You must be foolish to believe that someone would travel at night for over an hour to get drunk, let alone your own daughter. You know that I seldom drink," I said, infuriated.

She confessed that not only did she not believe me, but she was certain I was a "slut," because "people" said so. I got out of my room and walked to the kitchen for a drink of water, hoping to regain my calm. She followed me, continuing her accusations and condemnation of my misconduct. The confrontation was irrational.

I poured water in a glass and drank part of it. When I turned around, Mother was so close to me, I could feel her warm breath on my face. She was as angry as a bull in front of a matador's *muleta*. And in that moment, I was the muleta! The more I moved, the more irritated she got.

"Enagsek ala oumrik!" she yelled. May you be stripped of your life!

"When are you going to die so I can enjoy some peace in my life?" she said, looking up as if beckoning Allah for help.

For the bright young lady that I was, every time the woman who brought me into the world summoned the gods in my presence to sentence me to death was more devastating than I could ever express. So ample was the pain, if my emotions were audible, the universe would still be hearing my wailings to this day.

The pressure in my temples mounted, throbbing against my scull. I had a sensation of smoldering smoke emanating from my ears. I was transforming from the muleta into the bull. The rejection filled me with such a bursting rage that I wanted to die at that moment to serve Mother's desire to get rid of me.

I looked at the counter and saw a fruit knife on a white wire basket. I swiped it up and handed it to her. She grabbed it with no hesitation.

"Kill me!" I shouted as I ripped open the bone-white buttons of the dark-blue shirt that hugged my slim torso and exposed my chest to the blade she held. I was determined my life would end by her hand, so she could live ever after with the bliss of having eliminated me from her life, yet repentant for having killed me.

She stood in front of me. Her eyes glazed, and in the abyss of the short distance that separated us, I saw a thin sparkle of light on the edge of the blade as it came closer to my chest.

"Kill me! Kill me!" I kept begging her as I walked backwards away from her, tears flooding my cheeks.

"What are you doing woman? Are you crazy?" resonated the voice of my father through the electric vibe of the kitchen.

He grabbed Mother's arm by the wrist and pushed her away from me.

"Ente majnuneh?" he kept saying. Are you crazy? "What am I going to do with you, woman?"

I remained there, pinned to the kitchen wall, immobilized and mute, as I witnessed the fight that unfolded.

Their fight carried me back to reality. They were fighting because of me. Once again, Father saved me from Mother's claws. But I was ready to give my life at that instant of weakness, or defiance. I never reflected on the motives of that disgraceful incident. Was I depressed and suicidal and wanted Mother to be responsible for ending my life? Or did I want to prove to her that I would have died for my freedom as a young woman living in a society that rejected me?

Father threw a kitchen cloth at me. "Cover yourself, my daughter!"

The cloth landed on the floor. I blinked, held the two sides of my unbuttoned shirt close to my heart, covered my breast, and shook my head as if awakening from a frightening nightmare. I realized how my relationship with Mother was a sequence of horror stories. I walked away and locked myself in my room until the next day.

Mother's accusations based on rumours continued for as long as I lived in Syria. She never disclosed who the do-gooders were, but she always believed their contrived stories about me.

Giving Voice to My Silence

The last physical aggression I remember from Mother must have happened when I was 23 or so. Although I do not recall the exact reason for her tantrum that day, I do recall that she was running after me, carrying a chancleta in her right hand, along the 12-metre-long hall that separated all rooms and led to the front door.

I wanted to exit the house to prevent her from hitting me with the chancleta, as she did when I was a child. I opened the metal entrance door, painted in blue and pale yellow, and ran along the front porch. Before I could reach the six marble steps that led down to the long driveway, I took a violent hit between the shoulders as her chancleta landed at the base of my neck. Mother had a strong arm. She never missed a punch whenever she went through an episode of rage.

Besides the severe physical ache between my shoulders, I was so ashamed, as our neighbour across the street, a young man slightly older than me, was standing on his balcony. I knew he had witnessed the whole event, and that made me feel so inferior and embarrassed.

In retrospect, I realized it was not me but Mother who should have been embarrassed. It is typical of abusers not to recognize that their behaviour is unacceptable and for the victims to carry the shame of their abusers. But the most embarrassing truth is that the abuser was my own mother, the woman expected to protect me the most. I always feel envious when I see or meet people who have loving relationships with their mothers and wonder how my life would have evolved had my relationship with Mother been different.

Montaha Hidefi

Chapter 19

After Mother, the second biggest offender, the one that continued what Mother started, was Charles.

Shortly after my arrival in Montreal, I realized it was difficult for a "landed immigrant," as it was referred to then, to find employment. Interviewers wanted to hire individuals with Canadian work experience. How would a landed immigrant build any experience if no one offered an opportunity to start somewhere?

To build my Canadian work experience, the first job I could find through the unemployment office was at the Centre for the African Arts. The centre was a government-subsidized program that allowed the founding group of individuals to import art pieces of low to medium value from African countries and sell them locally. I was the only employee with a master's degree among the other "landed immigrants" and local Quebeckers employed by the centre.

At the start, it sounded like a perfect opportunity, as I loved the arts, but soon I understood it was not a place where I would build a career. The government was about to stop the subsidies, and I was looking for another job. But at least then, I could say I had a Canadian work experience, even though it was only about two months. The only task I performed was to clean the African masks and other objects on display.

I then found a part-time evening job as a telemarketer. My duties required me to call television viewers and read scripts on a computer screen to ask what program they were watching at that specific time and what they thought of the program. It was a disappointing job as most times people hung up on me.

I looked for another job and enlisted with various recruiting agencies. Soon after, one lady at a recruiting agency was incredibly positive about my chances for an office assistant position she was trying to fill. She asked me to show up one morning, and she would provide me with instructions and the address of the company where the owner would interview me.

I was at her office by the prescribed time and waited for her at the reception. More than an hour passed, and still I waited. I asked the receptionist for information about the delay. The recruiter came out and asked me to her office and told me, with disappointment, that the owner of the company was Jewish and that he wanted to hire a Jewish person, which meant that I was no longer a candidate. She apologized for the inconvenience and said she would get in touch about any other upcoming opportunity.

It was a smack in the face, and a very painful one. I wanted to understand the rationale behind it and realized it was discriminatory. I was troubled. Out on the street, I went to the first phone booth and looked in the Yellow Pages for the address of the Human Rights Commission in Montreal. I took the bus, went to the office on Saint Jacques Street and filed an official complaint. I was determined not to accept this form of bigotry.

A couple of weeks later, I received a letter from the recruiting agency requesting that I attend a meeting in their headquarters. During the meeting, the recruiter and her superior explained that they received an official complaint from the Human Rights Commission and wanted to find out what I would accept in exchange for dropping the complaint. Looking back, they were trying to eliminate any traces of human rights infringement, as that could affect their operations. I also thought they wanted to ensure I did not ask for financial compensation.

Humorous as it might have sounded to them, all I asked for was an official written apology and an opportunity to seek employment. I just wanted to find a suitable job and did not think of financial compensation.

A week later, I received a letter of apology and soon after went to the Human Rights Commission and dropped the complaint. I never heard back from the agency.

Through newspaper announcements, I found two opportunities where employers were interested in my skill set. One of these was as paralegal assistant at a lawyer's office and the other as office assistant at a shop for refurbishing industrial valves. I decided on the latter as I did not see myself in a law firm.

When I started working at the refurbishing shop in Pointe-aux-Trembles in easternmost Montreal, I kept my evening job as a telemarketer until I felt comfortable with the new job with Charles, the owner.

The shop was a messy space with a vast number of machinery and equipment at the back of a modest and disorganized office. Charles, a non-academic, outgoing, handsome man, was sharp and clever and always well-informed since he read the daily newspapers from the first page to the last. He had a striking personality and portrayed self-confidence despite his unhappiness with the shop and the high employee turnover. He spoke loudly on the phone and addressed the shop employees, who were partly "landed immigrants" and partly Quebeckers, with indifference and contempt because he thought they were not performing well and were stealing from him.

He saw me as a rescuer and tasked me with varied responsibilities, including accounting and data processing, even though I did not have any experience in either. He pushed me to try my limits and learn through practice.

On Thanksgiving eve, he asked me if I would like to accompany him for dinner at his mother's in Saint-Anicet, a small town an hour-and-a-half drive southwest of Pointe-aux-Trembles.

I did not have anything else to do for the holiday, my first Thanksgiving in Canada, so I accepted the invitation, as he promised to drive me back to Montreal after dinner. However, we wound up having to spend the night at his mother's since he had indulged in too much wine and could not drive, and I did not have a Quebec driver's licence yet.

The evening, the dinner, and Thanksgiving Day were surprisingly pleasant with Charles and his mother at her rustic, cottage-like, spacious house. Everything went well, and I enjoyed my time. Charles displayed affection and charm toward me. I thought he was flirting. I knew he had an attraction for me.

Weeks after Saint-Anicet, Charles and I engaged in a little romance, and he asked me to move into his apartment in Pointe-aux-Trembles, near to the shop. I could save the CAN$350 I paid for the studio apartment I rented on Saint Catherine Street East across from Papineau metro station, in the heart of the gay village. I accepted since I had an affinity for Charles and our romance was developing in a serious direction.

A year later, we bought a small house in Repentigny, an off-island suburb east of Montreal, and we registered it in my name.

Charles drank a bottle of wine every night after work. His disappointment with how the shop progressed, created an elevated level of anxiety. He started becoming irritable and short-tempered. At the shop, he yelled at employees and called them "imbeciles." He also yelled at me when things were not going his way. Everybody feared him. None of us would respond with a single word when he was in such a mood. Over time, employees stopped showing up for work, and I was stuck among it all.

I felt entangled in the relationship with Charles, and I depended on him. He was the main source of living for me, as shortly after I moved in with him, he stopped considering me an employee but a family member and no longer paid me a salary for my work in the office. He would buy me the most expensive shoes and outfits, but only when they were on sale. The first time I travelled to the United States was with him. He paid for my first car, a second-hand, dark-red Chrysler. I would have been unable to afford the US$1,000 the owner in Vermont wanted for it.

As his dissatisfaction with everything heightened, our arguments increased. His verbal abuse amplified as time passed. He started blaming me for things that went wrong at the office. He said I was "an imbecile from Syria that did not know anything about life and work in Canada." In a sense, he was right that

Giving Voice to My Silence

I did not know much about Canada, but he was expecting more from me than I could offer, as I was new to the country. Before relocating to Canada, I was a translator and not an office manager. But my lack of knowledge about working standards in Canada did not mean that I was stupid, nor did it give him the right to insult me.

One day in the office he was so upset about something, I do not recall what, he became hysterical. He pulled me by the arm and punched me on the left shoulder while yelling out his usual French Quebecois profanities, *"Osti, câlice de tabernak!"* and *"Criss câlice de tabarnak!"* which meant something like "Jesus fucking Christ, there's no way you can be this stupid." He reminded me of Mother.

Unable to defend myself otherwise, I left the office, announcing I was going to the police station of Pointe-aux-Trembles, only five minutes away.

As I was trying to explain the situation to the female police officer, it muddled me to see Charles entering the police station with a big smile on his face. He asked that I go back with him. I was so scared of the repercussions, I did not file any report for domestic violence, even though the police officer encouraged me to do so.

I had to contemplate my options. I did not know how to react or where to go if I filed a report or left the house.

He was tender, loving, and affectionate the days that followed, as if nothing had happened. I thought the physical violence was only a phase and that he would go back to being normal.

As the months and years progressed, his mood swayed often. Sometimes he would be calm, and others he would get enraged like an angered dog. Although he did not consider himself to be an alcoholic, his alcohol intake amplified in the evenings, and he drifted away from reality. He considered me as his relief valve. He directed all his rage against me. He did not spare any occasion to punch me in the face, arms, or chest. I had bruises everywhere and always tried to hide them. I was ashamed. I could not tell anyone about the physical abuse. Besides, we had no friends. He had me isolated in his little kingdom. I felt humiliated. I was reliving the events I had with Mother.

One weekend, he planned to fix the wooden fence. He asked me to drive to the shop to pick up the wooden slats he had stored there. He attached the trailer he had leased to the car, and I drove with one of his employees who was helping him. On the way back, contrary to the instructions he gave me, we took the highway. Driving at slow speeds pulling a trailer on the highway was against traffic rules. As he had anticipated, the trailer began to sway, and a police patrol stopped me, fined me CAN$80, and asked me to turn back and take the side road.

When we got home and I told him what had happened, he was so angry he punched the bedroom door, leaving a well-rounded hole that remained there as a memento of that unusual yet typical day.

On another occasion, in a moment of anger, he punched the dining room wall, near to the bedroom door, leaving yet another hole as evidence of his violent, physical reactions.

Charles lived in a world that existed only inside his head. He lived detached from reality and in denial of his situation, until one day he read an article about chemical imbalance of the brain and how that resulted in anxiety.

He decided to see a psychiatrist. The psychiatrist diagnosed him with bipolar disorder and an advanced case of depression. He prescribed antipsychotic medicine including Prozac and other opioids. Charles started his medication, but his situation did not improve. On the contrary, he became more violent, and I was scared for my life.

I packed my bags more times that I could count but did not leave. I did not know where to go. I felt imprisoned inside a Canadian horror story and did not have anyone to talk to. His situation worsened by the day, and he started to hoard whatever he came upon. Our house was filled with piles of magazines and newspapers, it was hard to find a way through.

Giving Voice to My Silence

The psychiatrist changed the doses of his medication more than once, but the violent episodes persisted.

I had become miserable and isolated from the outside world. I did not have friends or family. I could not talk to anybody about my situation. I only left the house alone to go to the office, and from the office I went to the bank or grocery shopping. Once a week I made a trip to Alburg in Vermont, to pick up his mail from the United States. He had a green card and received work-related mail at a post office box in Alburg.

One afternoon at work, Charles had to go into the city and left me in the office with the financial controller, who visited occasionally to check the books. He had noticed Charles's verbal hostility toward me. He asked me if I was all right.

"Yes," I said. "Everything is fine."

He did not believe me. He continued asking questions until I came clean and showed him the bruises on my arms and cried.

"You have to get out of there," he insisted. "You cannot stay with a person like that. You do not deserve this."

"Where can I go?" I replied. "I have no one."

"There are special houses for women in your situation," he said. "Let's find one in your area."

I had no clue about what he was talking. "Houses for women in my situation?" What did that mean anyway? He explained that domestic violence against women was a big problem in the province of Quebec. The government had sponsored houses to shelter women going through tough times like me, until they found a solution.

He searched the Yellow Pages for a battered women's shelter in Repentigny and found one close to our house.

"I'd recommend that you leave today," he said. "Before Charles returns home. It is not safe for you to stay."

After five o'clock, I locked the office and went home. He was not back yet.

I gathered some clothes and other necessities in a plastic bag, wrote a brief note to him saying not to look for me, and left the house in a hurry.

I started driving toward the shelter. My heart rate accelerated to maximum speeds when I found out it was five minutes from our house. Charles would easily spot my vehicle parked in the street if he went looking for me. I could not stop. I was scared.

I continued driving until I reached the Les Galeries Rive Nord shopping mall. I parked there and stayed inside the vehicle. I was unsure whether I wanted to leave him or not, despite the abusive situation in which I found myself submerged up to my neck. Yes, Charles was violent and inflicted me with physical and emotional pain, but when he was calm, he was tender and affectionate. He had helped me over the previous three years, and I learned so much from being with him.

I stayed in the vehicle until the sun went down completely. I had chills despite the nice summer temperatures.

I had to make up my mind. It was one of the toughest decisions of my life. My existence as a human being was crushed, like a cockroach under a boot. If I returned home, I would miss the window of opportunity to get out of that mess and start a normal life. But I did not know what to expect if I went to the shelter. There were too many unknowns to overcome.

I was becoming hungry and tired. I turned the ignition on and drove without determining my destination.

As I reached the shelter, I pulled over and looked at the house. It was dark. All outside lights were off. I saw a hint of faded light behind one of the windows. It looked macabre.

I drove again. When I reached the next crossroads, I stopped, turned around, drove the block, and parked on the other side of the street, across from the shelter. I turned the ignition off, picked up the plastic bag, collected my shattered bits on that sad evening, crossed the street, and knocked on the door.

Uncertain of where that door would lead me, I contemplated how it was one of the most demoralizing yet most promising doors I had knocked on in my life. I was standing in front of

Giving Voice to My Silence

the cave of the forty thieves, and I needed the magic word to access it. I could not fathom the mysteries concealed behind it or the treasures I would find.

"Qui est là?" a gravelly female's voice demanded from behind the door. Who is there?

"J'ai besoin d'aide. Pourriez-vous ouvrir la porte, s'il-vous plait?" I replied with caution. I need help. Could you please open the door?

A commotion of clicks and clacks rattled behind the door while I waited in the dark. Each time I thought the door would open; I heard more deadbolts sliding over. It felt as if they were unlocking an ancient citadel's gate, and hundreds of soldiers wearing invisible cloaks were watching my movements, waiting to pierce my skin with arrows if I made one wrong move.

A moment of silence followed before the door cracked open. I saw one eye peeking from the dim light that appeared through the crack.

"Qui êtes-vous?" the woman asked. Who are you?

"My name is Montaha. My boyfriend is abusive. I left the house earlier and I have no were to go. Could you help me?"

Skeptical, the woman scanned me from top to toes with doubtful eyes, while two other women appeared behind her.

"Entrez, entrez!" she said, making room for me to enter. Come in, come in!

I stepped in, hesitant, as if walking myself into a prison. The tumult of the deadbolts' clunks repeated behind me, while the two women asked me to follow them through the gloomy living room, into a room that served as an office.

I was so tired and scared I do not remember the number of questions they asked me as one of them filled out the forms she pulled from a drawer. They explained how fortunate I was as they had space for me. They showed me to a room, turned the light on, and pointed out the bathroom down the hall. They instructed to disinfect the toilet after each use as a courtesy to the other women occupying the house. They mentioned there was macaroni leftovers in case I was hungry.

In the corner of the beige room was a single bed covered with a red-and-black, checkered fleece blanket. Next to the bed was a wooden side table with a lamp on it. The blinds on the window were drawn. I threw the plastic bag and my purse on the bed and followed the women to the living room where they introduced me to other women sitting there, watching television. I felt a chill run down my spine.

I retired to my room without eating the leftovers offered. I always liked to prepare and cook my own food and did not rely on ready-made dinners. Once I was alone, I sat at the edge of the bed and felt like a warrior that retreats to a bunker. I was exhausted. I immediately felt the fibres of the fleece blanket itching my thighs through my pants. I had always been sensitive to this type of fabric.

I did not sleep the entire night, thinking of Charles and how upset he would be after discovering that I left. I was less than comfortable with the fleece blanket and the thought of sharing a bathroom with other women I did not know and eating food I did not usually consume.

I got up early the next morning to use the bathroom before anyone else. The lady supervisor was already preparing coffee in the kitchen. I had to sit with her later to go through the overwhelming shelter rules. I thought it would have been better to call them prohibitions. The list of forbidden things included opening the window blinds, turning the lights on at night, leaving the toilet and shower undisinfected after each use, leaving the kitchen dirty after each use, avoiding collaborating to maintain the common areas of the house clean and tidy, parking a vehicle in front of the house, going out unless permitted to avert an encounter with the abuser or prevent him from finding the house, watching television or listening to radio with high volume, using the telephone to contact anyone, getting up, sleeping, and eating outside the prescribed times, and most importantly, being absent from the sessions provided by the supervisor to raise awareness about abuse. I was in a safehouse, which is what a battered women's shelter is.

After two days, I was tired of sharing a common space with other battered women and listening to discussions about physical abuse while their children played and yelled. I was missing my own quiet house, my kitchen, and my clothes. I missed going to the office and feeling productive. I was missing Charles and my life with him.

I asked permission to go to the mall for fresh air. While at the mall, I called Charles at the office. He was calm and mild, and we had a decent conversation. He asked me about my whereabouts, and I told him that I was in a shelter. The conversation was short, but it was the first time in two days I spoke to someone who understood me.

That evening around nine o'clock, while we were all sitting watching television, the telephone rang, and the supervisor announced it was for me.

I took the handset and said, "Hello?"

"Salut mon bébé, comment ça va?" Charles asked. Hey baby, how are you doing?

I almost fainted. I wondered how he knew I was in that specific shelter, but knowing how resourceful he was, it was easy to guess.

I was embarrassed as everybody in the shelter was looking at me and listening to what I was saying. I told him I could not talk and ended the conversation.

To the dismay of the supervisor, and as per safety rules, I could no longer stay in the shelter. She allowed me, however, to spend the night there because it was late. My abuser was not supposed to find my location from fear of an eventual attack against the house. I had put the shelter in jeopardy by calling Charles from the mall.

The next morning, I got up, packed my things inside the plastic bag, and waited for the supervisor to dismiss me. I was surprised when she told me that because of lack of availability in the other shelters in Repentigny, she had found me a bed in a shelter in Montreal, at Le Plateau neighbourhood.

I was astonished by this sympathetic treatment. I spent the previous night thinking how I would survive back with Charles, but instead the supervisor found me a room in another shelter to protect me from the abuse. I was so grateful.

My move to a new shelter in Montreal was the key to my liberation from Charles and the path that allowed everything else that ensued in my life after that day.

Although the situation in the shelter in Montreal was not as good as the one in Repentigny, I met new women with whom I could talk and became friends with. One of the ladies and her daughters remain my friends to this day.

Through the weekly sessions in the weeks that followed, I learned about the four stages of the cycle of abuse. The abuse starts with the tension building between a couple. Mild or acute violence may follow. After an episode of violence, the abuser usually reconciles with the victim, and they go through a so-called "honeymoon." A period of calm happens after the honeymoon, where the couple enjoys their life again and the victim believes that everything is fine. According to Lenore E. Walker, who developed the social theory of the cycle of abuse after she had interviewed over 1,500 women subjected to domestic violence in 1979, there are patterns of behaviour in an abusive relationship, and the cycle goes in a certain order. Battered women like me needed to learn to recognize the patterns to prevent the abuse from happening again with another abuser.

Two months later, I moved to a small, subsidized apartment, sponsored by the shelter. I was able to pay the affordable rent through the modest welfare income I was receiving. I then looked for employment and found a part-time job as a sales assistant at a cleaning supplies and sanitation equipment company.

Chapter 20

During my graduation year from the University of Damascus in 1986, I had to find a source of income to support my daily expenses. Ruth's friends, two sisters from Turkey, were dating two brothers from an affluent Damascene family. They owned commercial stores at Al-Hamidiyah Souq. The arched, iron-ceilinged, six-hundred-metre-long souq was the largest shopping area in Syria, located inside the old walled city of Damascus next to the citadel. Dating back to the Ottoman era, the souq is one of the oldest malls in the world and it was always bustling with people.

The brothers recommended I have an interview with Fathi, an affluent Damascene businessperson who dealt with imports and exports and had an office in the souq area. He was looking for a secretary who spoke English to look after his correspondence with Asian countries.

I took a taxi to reach the office on Al-Asrouniah Street before the main entrance to the souq. When I arrived, there were no office buildings, only warehouses with steel doors rolled up, as the heat and humidity of the late afternoon were suffocating.

The address I had, matched one of the warehouses. I asked a worker about Fathi, and he directed me to take the stairs at a warehouse across the street.

To reach the staircase, I had to go through bulky packages scattered on the warehouse floor. At the top of the staircase was a cement structure supported by four concrete columns. It was apparent that the structure did not form part of the original warehouse and may have been added later.

As I walked up the stairs, a musty odour sprang from the open door.

The so-called office was dark, illuminated by the last rays of the afternoon sun coming through a big window behind an expensive wooden desk where Fathi sat. I greeted him with a handshake and introduced myself. He asked me to take a seat in one of the two luxurious, Damascene-style, wooden chairs in front of the desk. Piles of paper files and documents covered the desk, and a beautiful Persian carpet dressed the floor.

He told me he needed a secretary to work four hours a day, from 10 in the morning to 2 in the afternoon, to redact and type English letters addressed to companies in Taipei. In return, he was offering enough money for me to cover my expenses. He said I could start the next day.

Although my English was satisfactory, and I was familiar with typewriters, I did not know where Taipei was and had never composed a business letter before. However, I remained quiet because my main concern was to get the job. I thought I could learn new things while doing them.

For the next three weeks, I worked in the dark office upstairs seated at Fathi's expensive desk. Doing too little bored me, and I ended up tolerating the unpleasant smell of the wool and silk carpet, the damask furniture, and the stagnant air. After I organized the files covered with the dust of years past, there was little left to do. Most days I did nothing and did not see Fathi. I took advantage of the free time to study and do my homework.

When Fathi needed a letter typed, he would show up in a hurry and dictate the content in Arabic. I had to figure out how to compose it in English. After I had done this for a while, I understood the letters were not only addressed to Taipei, which, I found out years later, was the capital of Taiwan. Most letters were supporting import documents to help clear goods imported from Taiwan at Syrian customs. I once came upon a set of original documents and invoices from Taiwan, left the night before on the desk by mistake, and they showed figures and numbers that differed from the content I was preparing.

I deduced then that my role was to falsify import documents. I did not feel comfortable with this role and wanted to leave but did not want to cut the only source of income I had. I asked the same brothers if they knew about any other openings.

Days later, they recommended I call someone for an appointment as they were looking for a secretary. After I called, they provided an address to go for an interview. When the taxi arrived at the address, I found myself in a residential area in front of an eight-storey apartment building. I took the staircase to the second floor. There was no sign on the door, only the apartment number. I rang the bell. Someone that looked like a tea boy opened the door and allowed me in.

The hall was empty except for a big metal desk in the middle, a chair behind it, and a sofa next to the entrance. I saw other metal desks in two other rooms that had their doors open and noticed three men in one of them, deliberating about something.

After they concluded their meeting, they came out to the hall, and one of them invited me to enter the same room. He asked me to have a seat in one of the chairs in front of the desk.

The man was in his early thirties, well-dressed and well-manicured. In a Damascene accent, he asked about my experience. I told him I was currently employed but was looking for a better position. He had a smile on his face, so I presumed he was pleased with my qualifications.

He then said that I would get the job. However, he wanted to put forward a condition, so we could understand each other in advance.

"What condition?" I asked.

"Every Wednesday," he said, "you are required to spend time with me after three o'clock."

"To do what?" I asked.

"You know."

"No, sir, I don't know. Can you please explain?" I asked.

"I am a man," he added, while his smile became larger and his eyes flashed.

"Yes, I know, you are a man, sir."

"Yes," he continued, "and as a man, I have physical needs that need to be fulfilled."

"What type of physical needs, sir?" I asked candidly.

He looked at me with astonishment, as if wondering whether I was stupid or ill-advised.

"A man's needs are well known!"

At the realization that he wanted sexual favours every Wednesday, I contemplated a way out of the interview without the prospect of a sexual assault. We were behind closed doors. It would have been easy for him or any of the other men to take advantage of me. Even if I had screamed, no one would have heard. I was defenceless, and I needed to play it smart.

He was waiting for an answer, but all I could offer him at that moment was a pale face and a million-pulse-per-minute beating heart. I knew that despite my fear of getting raped, I had to keep my composure and behave as if what was happening was ordinary.

After a long pause, during which I tried to locate the other men through my peripheral vision, I stood up slowly, sported a fake smile, and asked carefully, "Can I take some time to think about it?"

He stood up too, walked toward me, and replied, "I need an answer tomorrow, because I have other candidates."

"I will call tomorrow," I said, and shook his hand.

I turned around cautiously. I did not want to give him any opportunity to grab me from behind. I walked out of the room slowly while looking around to keep the other men in sight. One of them was sitting at the desk in the hall. I walked toward the door. I turned the handle and propelled myself outside, slamming the door behind me. I ran down the stairs to get out of the building before someone followed me.

When I reached the sidewalk, I stopped for a moment and puffed the air out of my lungs. I hurried away from the building while looking behind me to make sure nobody followed me. I hailed a taxi and disappeared from the neighbourhood.

I remained shaky for the days that followed and could not grasp the inappropriate openness of that individual during that interview from hell. I was, nevertheless, grateful that he had the audacity to bring such a condition out upfront during the interview rather than wait until he hired me.

I never called back and resigned from the other position at Al-Hamidiyah the same week.

Montaha Hidefi

Chapter 21

Each culture carries its own customs and traditions through generations to preserve its norms and practices. Trying to learn a culture for the sake of understanding it and being born to that same culture and not understanding it, is like navigating a deep, wide ocean. One could never guess how unforgiving the waves would be.

Unless a person is born to an Arabic family, it is difficult to understand the intricacies of being a female, and to comprehend the social responsibilities conferred upon females of Arabic descent.

After I decided to stay in Dubai in 1997, Dubai residents, originally from Al-Sweida, tried to contact me, as was customary to do when a member of the same community arrived in a foreign land.

As soon as my cousin Domingo, son of Tio Salman, who had by then married and was working as a teacher in the Emirate of Al-Ain, knew of my whereabouts, he got in touch and invited me to his house.

To get to Al-Ain, I drove for about an hour in my brand-new, red Chevrolet Cavalier, which I bought after my employment in Jebel-Ali Free Zone. Domingo and his wife were very welcoming. His wife prepared lunch. They had two kids, a girl, and a boy. The girl was around 12 and the boy around 5. I remembered when his wife was pregnant with the girl, while we were still in Syria. I remembered having held the girl when she was a baby as I visited her various times. I enjoyed and appreciated the reconnection with my cousin and his wife and promised to return as soon as I could.

On my way back to Dubai, I recalled how, after relocating to Syria in 1972, and moving to our new house, 50 metres away from Domingo's, the following year, he employed a deplorable tactic to make me surrender to his tricks, with the objective of winning me as his girl.

He was eventually just trying to fulfill the promise Tio Salman made when we were kids. He must have been 15 at the time.

One day, I had been at Domingo's house until darkness had fallen. He insisted on accompanying me home, although I thought it was unnecessary.

As soon as we started our short walk he said, "I am going to give you a riddle; if you can't solve it, you have to give me something."

"What thing?" I asked.

He hesitated and then replied, "A kiss!"

I was unable to solve the riddle since my Arabic language skills were not good then.

When we approached the back door of our house and before I could knock for someone to open, he held my arm and forced me toward him, trying to steal a kiss. I struggled to push him away and denied him the kiss.

Alarmed by the unexpected molestation, I knocked at the door, shaking. He walked away into the dark muttering, "You owe me a kiss."

When the door opened, Mother asked if something had happened because I was pale and looked strange. I told her everything was fine.

That was the first time someone had tried to force me to kiss. Since I had not kissed anyone before, I was agitated and terrified. Mother always advised us not to let men touch us.

The next morning, Tuesday, May 14, 1974, an unforgettable date on the calendar of my life, when I went to the bathroom, I found myself bleeding. I was shocked and thought it was a consequence of the violent way Domingo wanted to kiss me. I presumed that this was the act of rape. I cried alone in the bathroom. How would I tell Mother that Domingo had raped me the night before?

The bleeding would not stop. I went to the kitchen and had the courage to tell Mother. I could not believe how happy she was! She told me that it was my period, that this happened to all girls, and that it meant I had become a woman.

After that night, I stopped going to my uncle's house alone, to avoid solo encounters with Domingo.

I felt uncomfortable and was scared that he would try to kiss me again. I always thought I would faint if a boy kissed me or touched me in a romantic way.

The next time I drove to Al-Ain to pay a visit to Domingo and his wife, I enjoyed the gathering and the food his wife had prepared. It was a nice family get-together, and I thought I should visit more often.

When it was time to leave, he accompanied me to my vehicle. I thought that was out of kindness, and I appreciated it.

As I opened the Cavalier's door, he stopped me and said, "Montaha, I want you!"

"What do you mean, you want me?" I asked.

"I want to spend time with you," he said. "And by the way, you still owe me a kiss!"

Over twenty years had passed since the riddle trick. I was shocked that he had not let go, since he was married and had kids.

I was concerned. "You are my cousin," I said, "and you are married. This is inappropriate."

He painted a shy smile on his face and said, "I will have that kiss, no matter what."

Distressed, I hurried inside the vehicle, closed the door, waved to him, and left without looking in the rear-view mirror.

As I drove away, I tried to make sense of the situation but could not find any excuse for his behaviour. It wounded my feelings. I felt betrayed. His role, as my cousin, should be to protect me, not to make sexual advances, I told myself. I remembered how Tio Salman had promised me to Domingo and how I never had feelings for him other than being a cousin or a brother. My absence from Al-Kafr for an elongated period, first to train in France and later to live in Al-Nabek and then in Damascus, could have been the reason I did not end up marrying him. I grew up distancing myself from him as a potential husband. In addition, Tio Salman never mentioned the promise after we relocated to Syria. With all my knowledge of the Syrian society and the male mentality, I promised myself I will not marry a Syrian man, and not my cousin. I always imagined that if I married a Syrian man, he would stab me to death in my sleep. This image had traumatized me.

To avoid a similar confrontation, I waited awhile before visiting them again, hoping he would forget or apologize next time he saw me.

However, the situation repeated at the end of my next visit to his house.

"This is inappropriate," I said. "You are married and have children. You should not be doing this."

"You should not worry about my wife," he said.

I left again in anguish, thinking how disgraceful it was that I could not enjoy being with my cousin and his family without having him dreaming of me as an object of pleasure.

I was powerless and understood I would not be able to change his mind toward me. I could not tolerate going through this every time I saw him, so I decided to not return to their house again. I disassociated myself from them. When they called, I did not answer the phone.

I had other cousins in Al-Ain too. They were my direct family in the United Arab Emirates, and I wanted to build a healthy relationship with them, but Domingo spoiled everything with his murky mind.

My other cousins continued inviting me to visit, but I never went back to Al-Ain to visit them. They never knew the reason, and I wanted it to remain that way. It would have been too troubling for Domingo's wife, and she could have left him or not believed me, had I told her. The best option I had then was to stop the madness by disappearing from their lives.

I have not seen them again. It has been over twenty years.

Chapter 22

At the beginning of 1971, as the second semester of my sixth grade started, my skinny figure was gaining length, and my love for drawing and painting was growing. At home, I developed an interest in gardening and started cultivating a private garden in an arid part of the immense yard of our house in San Fernando.

I was further isolated. I only had one friend at school, Cristina. She was from Spanish origin, was the tallest girl in the class, and the eldest. She had fair skin with smooth, pink cheeks, bluish eyes, and golden locks. She was the prettiest girl of the school, which was part of the Grupo Escolar MacGregor, the MacGregor Educational Group. She wore her black nylon belt loosened down the waistline over the white uniform. It gave her a slim allure. I thought she seemed like an angel and felt embarrassed and inferior next to her as my skin contrasted with hers. Cristina and Señor Elías, our teacher, were close. They exchanged tête-à-têtes during recess.

The second week of the semester, nurses were touring schools to vaccinate students due to an epidemic. (I do not know what the vaccine was for and was unable to find that information online.) One day, early after lunch, two nurses reached my classroom. The classroom was at the end of the open-air hall of the second floor with no real door, only an entrance. On the back side, there was no wall separating the classroom from the patio. Instead, the room overlooked the patio with its large almendra and acacia trees that provided shade and allowed the constant breeze to freshen the air. I loved the acacias with their striking orange-red flowers. When they bloomed between May and September, their five-petalled flowers resembled an emergency flare. The almendra leaves changed colour to reddish pink or brownish yellow before they fell in the dry season. The colourful trees contrasted with the black iron enclosure installed at the edge to prevent students from falling to the patio. The dividing walls of the classroom were covered with a very pale tint of green, and the soft tone of the four rows of individual wooden desks complemented the organic colour palette. The everlasting, equatorial, bright, natural daylight lit the classroom.

The nurses pulled two classroom desks to the front of the room and started calling us up to get the vaccine. As the teacher withdrew behind his desk, an unrestrained hubbub started rising from the students.

When they called my name, I left my desk and went to the front, sat on the assigned desk, and lifted the left short sleeve of my white uniform, as asked. The nurse soaked a cotton pad with rubbing alcohol from a transparent glass bottle and rubbed my upper arm with it. She took a glass syringe from a ceramic box resting on the top of the other desk and quickly poked my bicep. *"Ya está!"* It is over! she said.

This is how I remembered this event, but when I recently found a journal, I had maintained during therapy in Montreal in 1994, I was surprised to learn that the inoculation was in my back. We must accept that recovered memories may be less lucid, as the mind may alter the reality of certain events over time.

I stood up and walked toward my desk. A sudden buzz, louder than hundreds of flying cicadas, burst inside the classroom and everything turned black. When I opened my eyes, I saw the faces of students and one of the nurses over me. Scared, I looked around and saw a multitude of black shoes with white socks surrounding me. I was lying on the floor of the classroom. I lost consciousness and fell.

The nurse gave me a hand to stand up. I sat at my desk. The world around me was spinning. I felt dizzy, with a heavy head.

By the time the assistant principal, Teresa, arrived at the classroom to check on me, I was slightly better, but she suggested I go home to relax. Teresa asked me to take my belongings and follow her. Stumbling, I followed.

We went through the hall, down the wide wooden stairs, and across the middle court under the scorching sun toward

Giving Voice to My Silence

Teresa's office. It was a 10-minute walk, during which Teresa asked *"Tienes tu regla?"* Are you having your period?

I was only 11 and did not know what that question meant exactly, but I answered, "No."

When we reached Teresa's office, she asked me to sit down on a black office chair. It was the first time I had been to her office. There was a desk with a black telephone on it and various stacks of documents. Teresa asked if she could call my father to come and pick me up. I announced that we had no telephone at home. Teresa left the office for a little while. When she returned, she said she had arranged for one of the teachers to drive me home.

I followed the young teacher in silence. I did not know him. He seemed in his early thirties. We went outside the chain-link fence to the parking near to the gate. The teacher stopped next to a white convertible Jeep. Its black poles shone with the reflected sun. He asked me to hop in.

I opened the door and had to push myself up to reach the step. He asked me the address and started driving. It was the first time I had ridden in a Jeep. Despite the leftover buzzing inside my head, I felt so alive as the wind beat against my pale face. I was happy yet apprehensive of what I would have to tell my parents when we got to my house.

The teacher stopped the Jeep outside our store. We got out and entered the store. I was still staggering around. He explained to Father what happened and asked him to have me seen by a doctor. He said I could go back to school when I felt better, then he left.

I ambled inside to the family room, as if floating weightless in the air. Father followed me and explained the situation to Mother, who was in the kitchen. She came out to the family room and initiated her usual laments while moaning, *"Shou baddi a'amal fikun?"* What am I going to do with you? And imploring her typical, *"Enagsek ala oumrik!"* May you be stripped of your life!

I was so weak, I took refuge next to Danela, who stood up for me when she could.

In the following days, Father took me to be seen by the family doctor, Dr. Farias. Fainting was something that could happen after a vaccination, but after examining me, he requested a blood work. The results showed I was suffering from iron deficiency and an extreme case of anemia. Dr. Farias recommended a diet rich in iron, such as beef, liver, and eggs to regain my strength.

As I had never been Mother's priority, she was not providing me with the attention I required. I was also so stubborn, I would not eat the chicken liver she would prepare, as I was grossed out by the blood odour. I would eventually eat a fried egg every couple of days. Beef was too expensive, so we did not consume it very often and relied on chicken as the main source of protein.

My recovery was slow. Four weeks after the vaccine incident, I was still getting dizzy every time I stood up and had to remain mostly seated on the couch in the family room, next to Danela. Every time I felt I would pass out, Danela would turn on the grey, square, industrial fan Father had acquired the previous year during one of his trips to the Llanos, the plains, to sell the cauchos.

Eventually I felt better and decided to return to school. When I entered the classroom and sat at my desk, I passed out and fell to the ground. This time, though, I waited in Teresa's office until I felt better and walked myself home.

Although my family had imposed rules that prohibited me receiving schoolmates at home or visiting them in their homes, before leaving school, I planned with Cristina to help me catch up with the curriculum I had missed. Cristina requested that I go to see her at home, after school hours, once a week on Wednesdays. Mother and Father were unable to disagree, given the situation.

I did not know how to get to Cristina's house, so we agreed that Rangel, another girl in our class, would accompany

Giving Voice to My Silence

me the first Wednesday. Rangel and I met in the street and walked toward Cristina's house.

When we got there, Cristina was lying in a hammock on the side porch next to Señor Elías. I was confused because the teacher was at least twenty years older than us. I thought that he might be a distant relative to Cristina, but we did not know at school.

Cristina left the hammock, while the teacher stayed in it. He greeted us with a smile and asked me about my health and when I was planning to return to school. Neither he, nor Cristina, seemed at all bothered or embarrassed.

Cristina gave me her notebook, and I left without comment but continued thinking about the awkwardness of the scene in the hammock.

The following week when I went to Cristina's to return her notes and get new ones, I saw the teacher again in the hammock lying next to her. We exchanged greetings. I got the notes and left.

When I felt better around the end of the semester and returned to school, I asked Cristina about her relationship with the teacher. She smiled and said, "I love him."

I was a child, too young to entertain the gravity of the situation between Cristina and our teacher even though it was normal for young girls in San Fernando to have boyfriends and get pregnant while still going to school. Not for us though. Mother and Father would have killed me if I had a relationship with a boy in those days. Girls of Syrian descent were destined to be married with Syrians and not engage in relationships before marriage, especially not with Venezuelans.

Montaha Hidefi

Chapter 23

As I was growing up, I continued to be called Negra by Mother's half-brothers, Tio Salem and Tio Nassar, and Tio Salman and other Arab friends of the family, such as Tio Abdo, Tio Atallah, and Tio Jad'an. Tio Adnan called me "Nazeeha," which bothered me because it alluded to me being my cousin Domingo's girlfriend, since his name was Nazih. Tio Adnan was a handsome young man with whom I was madly infatuated as a child. This kind of attraction to an adult is called teleiophilia and is common. Tio Nawaf also nicknamed me *China comunista*, communist Chinese. No clarification was ever given to explain this tag, but I had attributed it to my resemblance to Asians with my double eyelids, and my dark olive complexion. The nicknames and labels made me feel different, not in a positive way but in a bizarre manner.

The ethnic remarks and my apparent contrast to my siblings owing to my skin colour, the shape of my dark-brown eyes, large lips, and dark straight hair, made me feel and believe I was ugly and that, somehow, I did not belong to the family.

This conceived reality cemented my belief that Mother hated me for all those reasons.

Growing up with this conviction was dangerous to a girl like me. It led me to feel inferior among my sisters at home and my peers at school. At school, I was nicknamed *venado*, deer, by one of the teachers who lived in the neighbourhood, because "She runs like a deer during recess," she told Mother. After that, Mother reprimanded me and instructed me to be quieter at school.

Even though I was a Venezuelan citizen and spoke native Castellano, my fellow Venezuelans labelled me as *turca*, Turkish, and *mouseeuwa*, foreigner or alien, just because I was the daughter of immigrants, a Venezuelan branch of an Arabic tree.

In Venezuela, these racial slurs were commonly used to identify immigrants, regardless of their country of origin. *Mouseuw*, derived from the French *monsieur*, was used for males.

Mouseeuwa was for females. *Turco* and turca were used as if all Arab immigrants were from Turkey.

I was utterly confused about my identity. I was a black-Turkish-immigrant deer with Chinese traits. I had an extremely poor self-image. It was the perfect formula for a female under 10 to become the subject of abusive extortion.

In fifth grade, my classmate Rangel, who was referred to by her family name, was skinny, shorter than me, and had an elongated face with accentuated black eyes and dark complexion. She wore her long, straight black hair in a ponytail. Our classroom desks were next to each other, and we often spoke to one another. As the school year progressed, we started working on a drawing project together. I was comfortable with Rangel, maybe because we had various physical characteristics in common, and considered her to be like a friend.

One day, Rangel told me to pay her the 25 Venezuelan bolivars I owed her for the material we used for the drawing project we did together. I did not understand how exactly I owed her that amount of money. I knew I owed her two or three bolivars, but not 25. I tried to discuss it, but she was convinced and would not change her mind. "If you don't pay the money," she threatened, "my mother will go to yours and they will have a big fight." She then leaned closer and whispered, "You would not want this to happen, would you?"

Although not persuaded by Rangel's money calculations, I was torn between my fear of Mother and Rangel's threat. If I were to discuss this topic with Mother, I would be exposed to punishment and eventually I might be prohibited from going to school. I decided to keep it to myself.

The following day, Rangel insisted I pay her back. As I never carried pocket money, I told her I could not pay the 25 bolivars. She showed pity and made an agreement with me to accept instalments of one bolivar every day until the debt was paid in full.

To keep Rangel's mother from paying a visit to mine, I started stealing one bolivar, every time I could, from the petty

Giving Voice to My Silence

cash Father kept in the store in a cardboard box. The box was on a shelf, out of reach. I would keep a watch on Father until he went to the bathroom, then drag a chair from the sewing area, climb on it, reach inside the box, pick a bolivar, and hide it inside my notebook. The next day I would hand it to Rangel. This situation continued for a while. Even though I did not keep track of the money I was paying Rangel, I knew I had already given her over 25 bolivars.

As we started the sixth grade, Rangel came back asking for the balance of the money. I tried to convince her that I already paid in full, but her tone was menacing, and she insisted I needed to continue paying. I realized Rangel was extorting me but stealing money from Father's petty cash was easier than having to endure the horrifying reactions and punishments of Mother if Rangel's mother came to see her.

As I was walking to school one day, two or three months into the sixth grade, a group of teenaged boys was sitting on the elevated sidewalk of a bodega across the street from the school, watching the students. One of them, nicknamed Pelo e'Chucha, which means pubic hair, because he had an Afro, was sitting there with his bicycle leaning on the sidewalk.

As I passed by, my eyes mapping the ground from shyness, I heard him say, *"Esta carajita, cuando sea grande, va a ser bonita!"* When she grows up, this girl will be pretty.

I knew Pelo e'Chucha from the neighbourhood. He often rode his bicycle to run errands for his mother. He was tall and slim, around 15, with a dark complexion. We were not friends and did not usually speak to each other as we were prohibited to talk to the boys in the neighbourhood. Since I was extremely timid and considered myself ugly, based on the family's insinuations and all the labels given to me, hearing these remarks from Pelo e'Chucha made me feel euphoric. My eyes sparkled and a smile decorated my face.

This phrase continued to resonate in my mind every time there were insinuations about my looks. As if Pelo e'Chucha had the ability to peer into a crystal ball and predict my future,

I somehow believed that one day I would be pretty, and people would stop calling me names.

When I got to the classroom, Rangel asked if I brought the money. In an unexpected turn of events, I took the courage to say, "I am not paying you anymore. If your mother wants to come to talk to my mother, she can do so anytime."

"I will tell my mother!" she fumed. "You will regret this!" For the first time, I did not care about Rangel's threat. I felt invincible. I did not realize at the time that my newfound confidence was a result of the positive comment I heard about myself on the street that morning. The power of positive words and their effect on us are immeasurable.

Rangel stopped asking me for money, and her mother never paid us a visit. However, the extortion she subjected me to has remained etched in my mind, and when I think of it, it makes me sick.

The same year we left Venezuela, as I was coming of age, for mysterious reason, I was finally allowed to wear pants. It was then considered ill-mannered for girls from Arab origin to sport pants because they outlined the female figure, the shape of her waist, thighs, and genitalia. A decent girl ought to wear dresses only. The absurdity is that when we moved to Syria it was considered indecent for a girl to wear a dress and show her legs. Girls had to wear pants, even under a dress or a skirt. There were always unexplained contradictions in my life as a female.

I was given permission to go purchase a pair of pants. They were military green and made of corduroy, the thick, cotton fabric with velvety ribs that was trending in the early 1970s.

I was so happy; I donned my pants and went to have a stroll on the sidewalk around the store. Coincidentally, Pelo e'Chucha was riding his bicycle nearby. By then, when he was in the neighbourhood, he would wave hello to us.

I did not know how to ride a bicycle. I had only ever ridden the tricycle Hacinto had when he was a young boy.

I stopped Pelo e'Chucha and timidly asked if he would teach me how to ride. Danela and Yusra, who were watching, were scared that Father might appear at any moment and would shout at us, but I took the risk.

Pelo e'Chucha held the bicycle and told me how to sit on it. I jumped on the seat. He told me to put my feet on the pedals and showed me how to brake. He then pushed me forward.

The bicycle started gliding on the empty street. I was so happy, yet so scared. I was spontaneously able to control the wobbling bicycle and keep myself from falling. I rode to the end of the block. I loved how the breeze, generated by the motion, caressed my face, and made my short hair fly. Scared of making a turn, I stopped at the end of the street, put my feet on the ground, and turned the bicycle manually. I then mounted it again and rode back. When I got back, Pelo e'Chucha, Danela, and Yusra were applauding. I was overjoyed and forever appreciative to Pelo e'Chucha for allowing me the opportunity. I never knew his real name.

Those two major events that happened on the same day in my childhood, wearing pants and riding a bicycle, filled me with gladness I do not think I had experienced before. That one extremely joyful day in my unhappy life continued to put a smile on my face every time I thought of it.

Later in Syria, the belief that I did not belong to the family became a conviction.

When I accompanied Mother to visit relatives and other people in the village, people noticed my different appearance and always asked Mother where she "found" me. Although this kind of sarcasm irritated me, I mostly kept quiet and stared at the ground. One day, I was so outraged that I invented a story according to which, during her month-long voyage to Venezuela, Mother had a clandestine relationship with a dark-skinned Asian man on board the ocean liner, and I was the fruit of it. The story left everyone laughing, but Mother was offended. On the way home, she reproached my behaviour.

After telling that tale dozens of times in different settings, I began to believe that Father was not my biological dad. While it was a story made up to explain my different physical characteristics, it made sense in my mind and left me wanting to uncover the truth.

One day, I had the courage to ask Mother, "Who is my real father?"

Enraged, she replied, "What are you talking about? Are you crazy? Your father is your father! How dare you disrespect me like this?"

To prevent the situation from becoming more serious, I had to shut up.

Although I loved Father infinitely, my conviction that he was not my real dad was further reinforced when one day, in a hospital in Montreal, I was being treated for an unstoppable migraine and the doctor asked me if I was Asian. I was shocked! Out of curiosity, I asked her for the reason behind the question. She said that in the X-rays she noticed that the form and shape of the sockets of my eyes indicated I was of Asian origin.

Living for most of my life with the conviction that my real father was an unknown Asian man weighed on me. In 2019, I decided to take a DNA test to verify my ancestry. While I did not compare my DNA to Father's, the result came back indicating I was of Middle Eastern origin from the Levant region, which is in Asia Minor. I was a bit disappointed, as this disintegrated my fantasy, but I had to accept the fact that I had invented the story to explain my, until this day, inexplicably different appearance.

Chapter 24

In the first few days of 2021, during an online conversation with my sisters and Mother, she cried a lot, "Because I miss you," she said. She acknowledged how much she loved me and how much she admired my achievements in life. She admitted that she missed me so much, she asked God to reunite us in person one day before she died.

The sound of that unexpected confession, which I would not have imagined even in my dreams, gave me the courage to give voice to my silence. I asked her why she waited 60 winters to compliment me, and why she mistreated me as a child and even as a young woman. She could not believe what I asked. Crying, she denied ever hurting me. I reminded her of how she nearly suffocated me with her foot, and how she almost stabbed me to death. I reminded her how many times she hit me, how many times she did not believe me, and how many times she humiliated me.

To my dismay, she could not remember anything I was recalling. Many years had passed since the events of my childhood and youth, and she was old and weary of life. To my major surprise, she said with great humility, "My daughter, I don't remember any of these things. But if what you are saying is true and I did hurt you, I apologize. Forgive me, my daughter!" She swore by the God of the Druze that she loved me and appreciated me more than anyone else.

Her declaration reminded me of a letter of forgiveness I had written her many years ago but did not send. By asking for my forgiveness, she gifted me with her empathy and power. This new reality left me stunned. I burst into tears. I cried in pain, but also in relief. We all cried, Mother, my sisters, and I. The tears trickled down our cheeks like a balm, alleviating the anguish of the past.

Why did I wait so long to ask her those questions? Had I done it before, I would not have gone through so much suffering in my life.

Several months later, in the last week of April, I received news that the COVID-19 virus hit Mother badly. Someone must have transmitted COVID to her at home because she had not left the house for a long time. Her mobility was restricted to a wheelchair due to health conditions. My brother Hacinto, now a physician, provided her with all the necessary care to keep her alive. She suffered for two long weeks at home, during which she was hooked to a respirator, and her lips turned purple from lack of oxygen. She was in so much physical pain, all she wanted was to die. On the twelfth day, unaware of the passing of time, she asked when she would reach the 14-day mark, as she knew that the virus had a two-week survival term. We were worried and hoped that the infection would not be the reason for her last days.

Her situation kept me awake at night. I got up constantly to check for news on my cellphone.

About an hour before midnight on May 5, as I was watching a movie on Netflix, I had a vision that lasted a few seconds. In the vision, a young version of Mother rose from the shadows. She was wearing the same clothes she used to wear in the last years I saw her. She hovered before me, and then walked past me without looking at me, as if I were not there, even though I could see her face. She then disappeared into the darkness without saying a word. Upon returning to reality, I reckoned it was a farewell gesture. I was convinced she was about to pass away.

One hour after midnight, on May 6, only a couple of hours after my vision, I woke up from my sleep scared. I turned the cellphone on and saw the message I had been expecting for days: "What a sad morning! My Mother died" read my sister Rasmille's message.

Although I was not surprised, I was taken aback. I did not know how to react. I immediately called Mima in Montreal and broke the news. Mima and her family had been living in Montreal since 1996. My partner at the time, Charles, sponsored her husband, and they were all allowed to immigrate.

In the Druze community, the burial takes place usually a few hours after death and, due to the COVID situation, this was done even faster. With this in mind, we communicated with Rasmille by video via Messenger to see Mother one last time. They were dressing her body. Everyone was crying uncontrollably. Shaking, Mima was crying too. My stomach turned upside down, and I got the runs, not from disgust but from the severity of the circumstance.

With cellphone in hand, I sat on the toilet bowl, and watched in reverence the lifeless body of the old woman I once considered my jailer. I felt bewildered and drained of any emotion. I was infinitely disturbed by my abdominal reaction and the fact that I was bidding farewell to the deceased as I sat on the comfort station. I felt utter disrespect! But it was out of my control.

Eventually, I came out of the bathroom. Michael woke up to the commotion and joined me as we watched, in silence, the mortuary preparations live on video. I was unable to determine whether I was sad or hurt. I felt guilt, and anger because COVID had been transmitted to Mother at home.

I struggled to make sense of my feelings. Was I stripped of emotions? Or was I administered an intense, anesthetizing melancholy?

We stayed up the entire night. I was worried about Mima. She could no longer keep herself up. Her knees were failing her, and she felt frail from sadness.

A few days later, when Rasmille regained the ability to make conversations without sobbing, she recounted the agonizing, last 90 minutes of Mother's existence and her struggle with the departure of her soul at dawn in Al-Kafr. Surrounded by Rasmille, Hacinto, his wife, and my youngest brother, Nabil, Mother did not want to let go of life. At first, she made deep, inarticulate breathing sounds. She groaned and moaned repeatedly. She asked for Hacinto to massage the back of her neck and hold her head. She gasped. Her groaning weakened, and gradually turned into soft sighs. Then the sighs became intermittent and dimmer until she slowly, and with difficulty, exhaled her last breath. She groaned again and her head fell to the left.

The distressful account of Mother's last moments stood etched in my mind and left me even more confused and heartbroken.

In the days that followed, distinct images of Mother's corpse, decomposing in her final resting place, emerged in my head. I was making scenarios of the stages of deterioration. The first week of her passing, I imagined her belly bloat progressively, like a balloon, and then burst against the lid of her coffin. The following weeks, I imagined her face gently festered and consumed by maggots. I could not control this gruesome mind imagery.

The bewilderment persisted for weeks. I spent hours thinking of a past that included Mother and cried. My sisters and I comforted each other over video chatting.

Mother started appearing in my dreams. In each dream, she somehow extended a silent invitation to join her, but I did not accept. Perhaps it was my fear of death that triggered the dreams.

We had officially become orphans. Father, the man I loved and whom I considered my protector, passed away in August of 2018, following a two-day coma due to a fall on the entrance steps of the family house in Al-Kafr. He died doing what he loved most, walking around the house.

The process of mourning Father was beyond difficult. For months, a stabbing thunderbolt punctured my heart, and I tasted the bitterness of life.

Mourning Mother, however hard for several months, did not equate to the lost of Father, but it somehow debilitated my tenacity to keep moving forward. I was confronted again with the harsh reality, and the significance of life.

I paused the translation of *Groping for Truth: My Uphill Struggle for Respect* to Spanish, which I had started in February. It was tough to continue to translate and revise stories that involved Mother. When I resumed the work in August, for each story, I relived the events all over again, but somehow, I felt as if she were not in the stories anymore. I presumed I was disturbing her remains. However, my desire to share my story with the Hispanic community was deeper than the unforeseen anguish.

I know there is no true healing from losing a parent, even when the relationship was broken.

I managed to regain my strength, and the Spanish memoir, which included additional and updated information, as well as this new chapter, was published on December 17, 2021, with the title *Dando voz a mi silencio: mi lucha por el respeto entre Venezuela y Siria.*

My publisher, Anne O'Connell, then suggested that I also update *Groping for Truth*'s original manuscript in English and issue a new edition with the added material and the new title.

As always, I learned that after each fall it is possible to get up and continue the journey. Life goes on.

Montaha Hidefi

Epilogue

A person once told me that there were two types of injuries, physical traumas that leave visible scars on the body, and psychological traumas resulting from distressing events exceeding our ability to cope. The latter, accompanied most often with high doses of emotional devastation, produce invisible wounds that bleed in our psyche. As others are unaware of psychological injuries unless we openly speak about them, the trauma permeates, becomes debilitating, and eventually defeats us, while to others we might look healthy and happy.

As I reflected on this, I recognized the emotional impact of the mental and physical abuse I had suffered at the hands of so many, the way it bent my conduct and fractured my persona as I was becoming an adult.

For most of my life, I experienced a crisis of identity and felt I did not fit in any social order. Throughout my childhood, I was subjected to prejudice and racial discrimination in the country of my birth due to my family background. In Syria, the land of my ancestors, I was referred to as ajnabiyah, foreigner, because it was not my birth country. In my early years in Canada, until I became a citizen, I was a "landed immigrant." Later in Dubai, I was an "expat," while in the Netherlands I was transformed into a "highly skilled migrant." Somehow, I had been an immigrant my entire life, a *pájaro verde*, a rare green bird that did not belong.

While societies and governments rarely pay attention to the destructive mental effect these distinctive social statuses have on human beings, it is critical to highlight the profound ways in which they touch us.

As I lived with being regularly considered "not from here," it was impossible to have a sense of belonging to a specific nation or be comfortable among a specific culture. It was not until recently that I had identified with "citizen of the world." After many decades of being denied the sense of geographical belonging, "citizen of the world" gave me a harmonious feeling of fitting in. I came to the realization that instead of being accepted by a single nation, the world, however ordinary, became my country.

As I continued travelling, the concept of "home" became "home is where my pillow is." The world had at last reconciled with me, and I grasped the immensity of the notion of belonging. It mattered no longer what passport I carried and how others perceived me, so long as wherever I landed, there was a pillow I laid my head on at night that allowed me to sleep feeling content and accomplished.

I lived in distress for years, under the bulk of indignity and cruelty that resonated in my head, the conundrums I bottled up inside impenetrable urns in the deepest, darkest places of my inner self, and the deceptions of countless social injuries, false promises, and relationships with two-faced people that sought to satisfy their pride from the spring of my naïveté and trust.

There were times when the wreckage of my damaged persona was shattered on the pathways of life. I was weak, unconfident, and insecure. I felt undeserving and in self-defence, I became hostile. Consequently, to protect myself from the claws of society's crows and to guard the doves from my menacing attitude, I erected a sky-high crystal dome around me and sheltered myself inside it. I withdrew and preferred to be isolated. On occasions, I felt self-destructive and thought of putting an end to my life, but my determination to prove Mother and the world wrong kept me going.

As I battled in secret with low self-esteem, I was able to project strength and confidence. My determination to thrive and the creation of my imaginary toolbox contributed to help me keep my sanity and fulfill long-term goals that appeared far-fetched to many, specifically Mother. When she reported the rumours that made a "slut" of me, I constantly told her, and believed, that one day I would silence those rumours and the Samaritans would look up to me. Looking forward, into a distant future where I saw myself successful, kept my struggle for respect activated. The respect I deserved as a daughter, sister, cousin, friend, woman, and human.

It is worth noting that one day, when I worked at the embassy in Damascus, the phone rang, and the receptionist announced that someone from Al-Kafr was at the reception to see me. Though I did not recognize the name, and the man showed up with no appointment, I opted to see him. He sat across from me at my desk, and we exchanged the typical, long Arabic salutations. He then complimented me and said how proud it made him to see me holding such a position. He stressed that the purpose of his visit was to apologize, because in the past he had badmouthed me and considered me a "slut." I had proven the contrary, and he was sorry about his past behaviour, even though I was unaware of what he had said. It was the moment I had foreseen when I told Mother that Samaritans would one day look up at me. His unsolicited and well-intentioned confession was worth a million dollars. I felt gratified and accomplished.

My decision to seek psychological help, both before and while I lived in a shelter for battered women in Montreal, was a turning point. Through counselling, I found an expert, listening ear, readily available to hear my distressed inner voice with impartiality and guide me to comprehend again that there was a shimmering light at the end of the tunnel, emanating even from its darkest, inner point.

Before I left Charles, I submitted to unconventional music therapy. Once a week, I went to a clinic in downtown Montreal called Psycho-Physio, which no longer exists, and laid down for 45 minutes on some type of hammock hanging in the dark, inside a geodesic dome, while I listened to various music genres preselected by my therapist. After the session, when I was at home, I had to listen to the same music again. I kept a diary, as homework, to record all the thoughts that the music had evoked during the sessions at the clinic and at home. I also had to journal my dreams.

While reading this long-lost diary, which recently turned up in a box from the past, I was moved by how challenging the therapy was. During the first weeks, the treatment caused me much physical pain. I had headaches and felt as if my brain was being sawn in two. It also caused me back pain and anxiety.

At the end of the three-week therapy, and for many months afterwards, the therapist and I discussed my diary entries, and she analyzed each detail. Eventually, I was confronted with an ugly truth revealed by the therapist. Everything that had happened to me up till then was the consequence of having in my life the person who had brought me to life. Mother's abusive behaviour had overshadowed my character and affected me to the extent that I ended up attracting more abusive people into my life. That was one explosive discovery!

To benefit from the therapy, it was critical that I reconcile with Mother. The therapist suggested a phone call to openly discuss my feelings with her and, most importantly, to forgive her for all the harm she had inflicted on me. I was anything but ready for such an undertaking and did not think of forgiveness as medicine. How was I going to share my feelings with the woman I feared the most in the world? How was I going to explain to Mother that I had to go to therapy and that she was the source of all my problems? The alternative, suggested the therapist, was to write a letter of disclosure and compassion to Mother.

Writing a letter of forgiveness to Mother was the most demanding project I ever had to complete. I had to show clemency in recognition of cruelty. I had to exercise empathy in acknowledgment of condemnation. I had to convey love in gratitude for hatred.

I never mailed the letter to Mother. She would have been unable to read it because she was illiterate. However, the action of handwriting it was a symbolic victory over the wounds I had endured at the hands of my warden. It allowed me to recognize empathy, a quality with which I was unfamiliar.

Forgiveness, I learned, is an acquired virtue and one of the finest gifts I could offer others, as it infused me with power and allowed me to control my emotions. Although my last in-person encounter with Mother was in 1993, I did stay connected with her via video chats, and I do strongly believe that what she did to me was out of ignorance and lack of awareness.

To fulfill the second outcome of the therapy, I had to develop an action plan with the supervision of my therapist. By doing so, I learned that the most important thing was to have goals that were specific, measurable, attainable, and time-based. Looking back, I believe that having written my objectives with a concrete timeline, a practice I continued exercising during the ensuing years, supported my personal growth and crystalized my vision of the future. Knowing where we want to go in the future helps to make our actions concrete and eliminate any negative surprises.

Although most of the abuse in my life, and its scars, remained private until the writing of *Groping for Truth*, I am optimistic that by coming forward and sharing these stories, the scars eventually fade over time, though I know they will not vanish. The process of reviving every single detail of each incident, to be able to report it with integrity, was beyond overwhelming. It was like opening a time capsule and reliving the incidents one more time.

Many of the stories made me weep as I wrote them, and every time I reviewed them. There were moments when I wanted to stop writing, but my determination superseded the urge to stop.

I believe that when armed with determination, we can reverse the profound effects of any negative event by channelling our energy and transforming it into a roaring engine to empower our future. I found out that the best way to defeat an adversary was to outrun its capabilities.

Each time I faced a round of misconduct, I came out of it emotionally crushed but intensely more resilient, equipped with more strength and disposition to face the next one. As I look back on my life, I am certain the abuse, while uncalled for and completely reprehensible, was a catalyst that allowed me to unlock all gates to accomplish success.

My tenacious desire to improve the mental image of myself, created by Mother and by society, pushed me to seek education and knowledge to uncover and expose the person I perceived to be deep inside me. With perseverance and visualization, I bettered myself and attained goals beyond expectations. I speak five languages. I taught French to secondary grade students in Syria. I obtained three master's degrees from three different international universities. I fulfilled senior positions at multinationals in various countries. I immersed myself in the discipline of colour trends and forecasting. I have spoken publicly at international events, in-person and online. I translated from French to Arabic and published a book while in my late twenties, authored numerous articles published around the world, and co-authored chapters related to colour in two books. I have been, to date, to 59 countries. I trained in reiki. I have progressed with the meditation and visualization method of Silva Mind levels 1, 2, and 3. To top it all off, I even walked on fire while living in Dubai. All to overcome defeat and prove I could be the master of my own life.

In addition, the universe has blessed me with a loving husband who respects me and has supported me for as long as we have been together.

The process of authoring this book pushed me to go deep into the realm of my soul, to open doors long sealed, to unearth scars that profoundly marked my reality at the subatomic level, and to grope for truth.

While I seek not to minimize the effects and consequences of my struggle against injustice and abuse over the years, I came to realize that my fight was like chimes in the wind; their blowing tintinnabulations gave me the determination to overcome the wrongdoers, to keep looking forward, and the oomph to achieve victory over deception.

Giving Voice to My Silence

Though my stories might sound trivial to some, no injustice and abuse are to be considered insignificant or irrelevant. Only the targets of abusive actions can gauge their devastating consequences on their emotional lives.

This book is the new edition of *Groping for Truth: My Uphill Struggle for Respect* published in 2018. Along with a new title, in this second edition I included updated and added information based on entries from a journal I kept during professional therapy in 1994. I also added Chapter 24 to reflect on current times following the death of my parents.

This book is about the celebration of a human being that had to crawl through darkness to find light. This book is a celebration of Me. It allowed me a window through which I felt liberated of the burden I carried in silence for years. As I expose many wrongdoers by their first name, I realize there might be undesirable consequences. Nonetheless, I am ready to confront them all. I have been inspired by other individuals who stood tall against any pushback with even more horrifying and graphic stories of injustice and abuse. I am proud to join them in this journey with the aim to end the silence on all kinds of exploitation and shout "Enough is enough!" This book is an invitation for the silenced voices to speak up.

Montaha Hidefi

Acknowledgments

The process of writing and publishing a book is like going through pregnancy and giving birth. It requires the support of countless people and knowledge of the publishing process.

I thank all my friends and family members who accompanied and supported me during the process of writing the original English version, the Spanish translation, and the new edition of this book.

I am grateful to Anne Louise O'Connell, who supported me in writing and publishing my books.

Thank you to my friend Karl Rijkse whose casual encouragement of the idea for a book about the stories of abuse I went through was fundamental in the consideration of telling my stories.

I am immensely grateful to my husband, Michael Richter. There are no words to describe my appreciation for how he has stood by me with unconditional, emotional, and material support. I hope to be able to reciprocate his tremendous contributions one day.

Montaha Hidefi

About the author

Montaha Hidefi was born and raised in Venezuela to Syrian immigrants. When she was a teenager, her family returned to Syria, and as an adult she lived in the United Arab Emirates, the Netherlands, and Canada.

From an early age, Montaha found comfort in exploring the vivid colours of her tropical surroundings. She began writing during her teen years in Syria, confiding in a diary while attempting to process overwhelming culture shock and struggling to understand the upheaval in her life.

Through sheer grit and determination, she overcame huge obstacles to become a well-educated, highly respected businesswoman. As an internationally recognized colour archaeologist, she co-authored the first and second editions of *Colour Design Theories and Applications* in 2012 and 2017, edited by Janet West.

She has authored numerous articles related to her industry and profession for various trade magazines and websites. She is also an experienced trend panellist and contributed to the creative development of several trend books including *NCS Colour Trends* in Sweden, *MoOD Inspirations* in Belgium, and *Mix Magazine* in the United Kingdom.

Montaha has several advanced degrees, including an MBA, a master's in international business, and a master's in translation. In 1991, her Arabic translation of the French children's book, *Badang l'Invincible, Les Contes du Griot*, written in 1977 by Claude Duboux-Buquet, was published.

Montaha currently resides in Guelph, Ontario, Canada, with her husband, Michael Richter, a composer, pianist, and sound engineer.

Montaha Hidefi

You can connect with Montaha through any of her social networks:
www.montahahidefi.ca
www.facebook.com/montahahidefi
www.linkedin.com/in/montahahidefi
www.instagram.com/montahahidefi
www.twitter.com/colorfulmontaha

Designed by

www.ingramcontent.com/pod-product-compliance
Lightning Source LLC
Chambersburg PA
CBHW021446070526
44577CB00002B/274